YOU GOTTA ASK FOR
THE ORDER

YOU GOTTA ASK FOR THE ORDER

Life as a Successful Salesperson, Business Owner,
and Entrepreneur

STEVE CINA

"The Pessimist Sees Difficulty In Every Opportunity. The Optimist Sees Opportunity In Every Difficulty."

Winston Churchill

Introduction

> **"Everything you will ever want in life is already owned or controlled by someone else." Therefore, "Everything you will ever want will have to be negotiated for."**
>
> Zig Ziglar

I was 12 when I started my sales career selling candy and cookies door to door in Los Angeles. In her station wagon, Mrs. Colton would drive us kids to a neighborhood where she would drop us off and we would sell the candy and cookies to the homeowners. This is where my sales career got started. I learned then that all you needed was the nerve to *ask for the order*. If you don't ask for the order, no one's going to buy. They will not say, "Oh please, please, Steve, sell me the cookies." You gotta ask, "How many boxes should I write you up for?"

With the help of this book, your outside sales career will

improve by teaching you to go out and see the client instead of waiting for them to come to you. What do you think may have happened if I had stood on a corner with the cookies and waited for someone to buy them? That may have changed my life. I'm sure glad I went to them, door to door. I was Mrs. Colton's #1 salesperson from the first week and every week until I stopped selling sweets and cookies. I made about 50 dollars a week.

At a young age, I understood that you needed to *ask for the order* to succeed.

Have a Support System

COOKIES AND CANDY started my career in sales, but that isn't where it ended. I have had a successful sales career for over 47 years, and my experiences will help you to the top of your sales career, ultimately helping you get what you want out of life. If you learn from my experiences, you can reach any of your dreams and goals. It's all about dealing with all kinds of people, using common sense, making smart decisions, and *listening* to what they say.

You will need to have an executed plan that will help you adapt to any person's personality and situation to make a sale. I had a plan, and I followed it for over 47 years. I taught it to the salespeople I worked with. It worked for me! It worked for most of those that I trained, and it still does.

When I started my first business, I was 100% broke, but I knew that it would be a success. I just wasn't sure of just how fast and how large each business would become. There was never a doubt that I would succeed! My businesses in the chemical industry wouldn't have succeeded without my wife Virginia (Gine) and her influence in most of the decisions I made.

Virginia's boss, an acquaintance of mine, introduced me to Virginia. Well, Richard didn't really introduce us; he gave me her phone number and told me that his executive assistant was single and very beautiful. Like I always did, I went after the sale instead of waiting for it to come to me. I decided to go by his office and window shop her. I called her that night from my mother's home. Yes, I lived with my mother and stepfather George at the time. I asked her out for a drink. We met at a local restaurant on Interstate 5 and Newhall Ave. A short drink turned into dinner and a night of visiting. We started dating, and the rest is history. Virginia had a son, Morgan, who was 18 months old at the time. After a while, I adopted Morgan, and he became our number-four son. My family was, and continues to be, an important motivator.

Virginia was aware when there were important things going on and always helped me decide which way to go. In most cases, Gine did not tell me what to do, but she defended, respected, and supported all the decisions that I made. When we got into the specialty chemical industry, Gine worked the accounts receivable department. More importantly she built a rapport with the sales and office employees, and there was trust and respect. Over the years, people would frequently go around me and approach Virginia directly. Of course, she never got involved until consulting me, making the point that most of the time I was right. I ran the daily operations of the businesses and made most of the decisions based on the information that I had.

I once told Virginia that we were going to have a great life. We have had a great life, and in retirement, we still are. Retirement; what a joke! We are busier now than before, and it's fun. Thanks to the many people that have been our partners in business. Any successful business takes strong relationships and determination. Surround yourself with good people that can support you and help you achieve your goals.

Top Guns

IT MAY BE my Jewish or Italian heritage, or maybe it's both, but I always had an intense work ethic. Everything has to be done now! It must be done now, with the office team and sales team members. There was no doing it later; if you wanted to do it later, then you could do it with someone else-not my company. Whatever it was, if you were returning a phone call to a vender, or a sales-rep or a customer if you worked for me it was to be done now not later. This was the way it was. It worked!

If you were in the sales department, we gave you the tools and the support that you would need to be the best. We had a plan and a sales manual that explained in detail how to sell out products, most importantly our managers and trainers worked in the field with you calling on and helping you sell to your customers. We demanded that in the beginning you did it our way because our way worked. We promised to you that we would do whatever was possible for you to succeed, and we gave you 100% all the time, as long as you did the same. We knew if you weren't, and if you weren't, it was sayonara.

This was the way it was. It worked!

Flexibility came after you learned and mastered "Our Way." Then the sales team member added their own personality to the client relationship.

Every great sales company must have a tract (sales presentation) for you to run on, and ours was the best. We had the plan! All we needed was the right people to execute it, and over the years we found them again and again.

I looked for Top Guns. These were high performing salespeople who consistently brought in 80% of our sales volume. These people have high ethical principles, professional behavior, and they are fun to be around. They have an instinctual work ethic that can't be learned. Although they are rare, these people always stand out from the crowd.

If you want to find these natural leaders, follow these steps:

- **Don't hire sheep. We are looking for sheep herders.**

Sheep just fill a territory or slot. I have said in the past that most people are sheep. They are in a flock that moves from one place to another and follow the leader (herder) anywhere he may go.

Most companies today are content to hire people who have very little potential. We never hired just to fill a territory. When that's done, you will end up with salespeople who are mediocre at best. Howard Heller once told me, "Hire a piece of crap and you end up with a very well-trained piece of crap." Then we are stuck with them for longer than we would like, or we would be consistently turning sales reps. If we truly wanted the very best sales force, we knew that we had to coach them and provide the support necessary to make them the best they can be.

If we hired one of these mediocre people, after the initial training period had passed and they are not performing to our expectations, all the time you've spent training, educating, and sweating for that person is time taken away from searching, finding, and training a genuine top gun. Meanwhile, there is a top gun out there being hired by someone else. If the individual is not going to make it, make the change earlier than later.

- **Make sure your sales team can meet the demands.**

I was very demanding and expected you to work and go the extra mile on the job every hour and every day.

I also had the ability to recognize how far I could push each person and know when to back off. Some could not take it and left. It was not the right job for them. They may turn out to be good salespeople in the future with another company, just not with ours.

- **Conduct a thorough interview.**

If I interviewed you, within an hour into that interview I knew more about you than most people did after knowing you for years. I knew in that interview if you had a very good chance of succeeding with us. I have been told that I have the ability to pick the right person for the job most of the time. I tried to pass this instinct on to others.

In the interview, do the following:

- Ask good questions.
- See if you can get them to take over the interview.
- Ask why they think this is the right job for them?
- Ask them how they handle customer objections?
- Give them an object and have them sell it to you.
- Ask them what is their least favorite part of the sales process?

Know Thyself

SOME OF YOU have gone to college and worked hard to earn your degree. Congratulations and good for you. Now that you have your degree, what are you going to do with it? Most of you are not sure. Some take a job in the field they thought they wanted to be in, but then after a while, they say to themselves, "I am not happy. This is not what I thought it was going to be. I really want to do something else."

After family and friends tell you that you're a people person, you may say, "I want to go into sales." For those of you that said that, do me a favor and do something other than sales. Being a great *People Person* will not make you a great salesperson. I can't tell you how many people over the years I interviewed and hired that later changed their minds about what they really wanted to do. I worked in sales for all my life. I have had successes, and I have had my share of failures. It has been quite a trip that has taken me to many places, meeting people that have enriched my life. We all think about the short term that we have in this world, and at one time or another we all want to leave something. Be wise about what you change to and make sure it is something that you are passionate about.

Why is this coming out? I always said, "This business and job isn't for everyone." If it was, it would be easy. It's not easy; any sales career can be very difficult, and not everyone succeeds at it. But it is fun, especially when you have three sales in one day that total 3,500 dollars and you earned 1,120 dollars commission for that one-day working for us. It's rewarding when you discover your talent and how it can be put to use.

It is important to understand yourself and develop a passion for your work if you are to succeed.

I Chose to be a Salesman, or did it Choose Me?

I NEVER LIKED school very much, and as a result, my grades were not very good. I just didn't care. I liked gym and math the best, but the best class that I took was in the 7th grade. It was typing. Typing helped in just about every job I ever had, and I wouldn't be writing this if it weren't for the typing.

I was a high school dropout. I dropped out after going to three high schools in the Los Angeles area, and I did not make it out of the 11th grade. I certainly was not proud of this, but for some, school is not the most important thing in life.

When I was about 15, I worked the summer for my father. He was a plastering contractor along with my brothers, my uncles, grandfather, and cousins (most of them). My job was to mix the plaster by machine outside and shovel it on to the hod. I would then carry it on my shoulder to the plasterers in the house. I would do this all day. Two things did not go well: one, I was too slow for the plasterers; two, the job was too hard for a skinny little 15-year-old. I knew then that I was not going to be a laborer or plasterer. Not then, and not ever. This was working way too hard.

After a few other jobs, I was almost 18 years old when I left California and moved myself to Boston. I lived with my Uncle Harry and Aunt Josie. Uncle Harry was my favorite uncle and always looked out for me. He was a government meat inspector at the downtown meat-packing houses. He got me a job at one of the packing plants in Boston in the middle of winter. I started out pushing the hinds of beef out from the railroad cars in temperatures of zero to 30 degrees at 4 a.m. I moved them inside of the building where the butchers would cut them up. All 130 pounds of me would push a group of 10 quarter/hinds at maybe 150 pounds each. They were on rollers that led into the building. I soon got a promotion to cutting the kidneys out of the dead cattle. I think the promotion came from Uncle Harry persuading the owner of the packing house. It was worse than the plastering job! I decided then and there, no more manual labor for me. I was going to go back to California.

While in Boston, I met a guy that was a friend of my older brother; he may not have been the most honest person in the world, but I needed someone to travel back to California with me and share the cost of the trip. I had the car (a '56 Buick), and he had a credit card to help us get there. We drove and stopped in cities and towns frequently. It was fun, and at 17 everything stupid was fun. We did some stupid things; some were close to being illegal. He would steal license plates and put them on my Buick every so often. I asked him why. He didn't say why, and I guess I didn't want to know. He was five years older than me and had more experience than me, but I was game for almost anything. He knew a girl in Colorado Springs and wanted to go and visit her. We stayed at a motel, and she introduced me to one of her friends. Let's just say we had a heck of a time. Chalk it up to part of my growing up. After a few days, we were back on the road to California.

When we came to the sign that said, "Los Angeles County," we pulled the Buick over and tossed the plates that were on the car and put the California plates back on. It turned out the credit cards were stolen. Later in life, I discovered that this friend ended up in prison for a very long time. Once I was back in California, it was time for me to get a job and back to real life.

I think that sales chose me. Some of you may choose to be an accountant, a doctor, or a lawyer. I chose to be a professional salesperson. It gave me the opportunity to meet people from all over America and the world. I visited places that I never expected to see. It also gave me the opportunity to earn as much as I wanted. All I had to do was *ask for the order*.

I got to help the customers that I sold to. That's right! Salespeople help their customers. We make their jobs easier, so that they can be more productive by using our products. Most of all, we solve problems for them. Without our products, their jobs would be more difficult. I always told my sales team, "Become a **partner to your customer.** You work *with* them as if you worked *for* them."

Think Outside the Box

I was married at 19 and had my first son at 20. By the time I was 24, we had three sons. I had no choice; I had to work. One of my favorite memories involved saving soda bottles. Sometimes we were so poor that I would take them to the market and cash them in for milk for the kid.

I knew way back then, and throughout my life in sales

and teaching sales, you must have a plan. You must believe in it, be confident, know that there are no shortcuts, follow your plan, work hard and smart, and the rest will take care of itself.

When I was about 22, I got a sales job selling commercial truck tires for Sears and Roebuck. I was doing pretty good, then I landed the Lockheed Aircraft account in Burbank. I was selling tires that they used from little wagons, small utility vehicles, auto tires, truck tires, forklift tires, etc. It was great. I was doing well.

One day my boss told me that we were summoned to go to the Sears main office building downtown in Boyle Heights to meet some big shots from Chicago. I thought that I was going to get a reward or recognition for the Lockheed account.

I was wrong. They wanted to tell me that because of the great job I had done, they were going to make it a house account. They were going to take it away from me and our division. Thank you, corporate America!

I thanked them very much and told them to take the job and shove it up their ass. A few months later, Sears lost the account; they forgot the account needed constant servicing that could not be done from the office. You need to be in the field constantly working with the customer.

For a short time, I took a job working in my uncle Eddie's restaurant in the Pacific Palisades. (I had to make money). I would go in at 6 a.m. and make and bake the homemade pies for the day. After that, I waited on tables, allowing me to earn tips that amounted to about 30 or 40 dollars each day on top of the 90 dollars a week that Uncle Eddie paid me. Wow! Twelve hours a day, five days a week for about 200 dollars a week. I bought my first home on this job at this pay. I paid 17,500 dollars for a three-bedroom, two-bath home.

It was at the restaurant that I met a bunch of milk men that encouraged me to apply for a job delivering milk at Edgemar Farms. At 24 years old, I became a milkman delivering milk on the west side of Los Angeles. My route was in a very affluent area, including parts of Brentwood and Bel Air. Many of my clients wanted what was called an *inside delivery*. In other words, they allowed me to come into the kitchen and load the refrigerator with the amount of milk that they wanted.

Here is where I began thinking outside the box. I figured out that the customers wanted the milk, but there was much more that I could offer. I could offer them extras or additions to their orders, including eggs, bacon, butter, cottage cheese, etc. I bought the extras and set my own prices. I left flyers with my customers, and the orders for the extras started coming in. I did this for a few years. I would get up around 3 a.m., get to the dairy, load my truck, and drive to the route.

At 26 years old, I decided to buy my own route and milk truck and became an independent distributor. I was in business for myself for the first time. I continued to offer the eggs, bacon, bread, cottage cheese etc. and sold it to my customers. They loved the extras. I was the first to offer this from a milk truck; it just made sense to me. You need good common sense. My customers loved this added service; it made their life easier.

My route (territory) was in the San Fernando Valley nearer to where I lived in an area called Porter Ranch in Northridge, California. It was a new upscale housing development, and I was sure the homeowners could afford and enjoy home delivery milk service. They were going to build hundreds of homes there, and I was in on the bottom floor.

There were a few customers that came along with the territory that were in the foothills of the Porter Ranch development, but most people were moving into the homes as they were being built up in the hills. I spent a couple of hours in the morning making my deliveries and returned in the early evenings and weekends, spending my time visiting and signing the new home owners up for milk delivery. This meant I spent a lot of time sitting in my truck watching for the people to come by and see the progress of their homes.

After several months, my customer base (route book) would be so full that I hardly had time to look for new customers. I was relentless. I decided to sell some of my clients to other independent distributors in the area who didn't take the time to sign up new customers. I would do this and continue to open new customers and add to my client book. This went on for some time. I was willing to take the time and see the new people that were going to be moving into the neighborhoods. I delivered to them for a while, and then sold them to other milkmen for a large profit.

Now is a good time to mention my archrival, Greg Hoover. He was another independent milk distributor in the area, and he was under the impression that he owned the territory outright. He believed that no one else should come in. In fact, he once pulled a gun on me and told me to stop stealing his potential customers.

It all ended up fine; he and I became friendly. He did his thing, and I did mine.

I was just better at it than him. I was making a very nice living at this. Things were going well.

5

Make a Move When it's Time

MY NEXT MOVE, I bought a drive-in dairy in Van Nuys right by the Van Nuys airport. It was called Peter Pan Drive in Dairy. I had to wait for the customers to drive into the business. I tried advertising in the neighborhood with flyers; I put flyers on cars. I advertised locally, but waiting for the customer to drive into the dairy just did not work for me. This went on for about a year. I lost my shirt. Business was bad enough, and then one day a guy followed me into the office area, put a gun in my face, and robbed me. Waiting for the customer to drive into the dairy and order was not for me. I let the drive-in go back to Peter Pan. Once again, I lost a lot of money but learned my lesson, I think! It was time to pick myself up off the ground and start over again. I was 29 years old. I had a wife and three kids, a nice home, two cars, and a mortgage.

The milk business was great, and I did well. I sold my truck and customers and moved on to selling baby pictures. That's right. I sold baby pictures door to door and I get to go to the customer and not wait for them to come to me. No more waking up at 3 a.m. to deliver milk.

I had a neighbor whose father-in-law had a photography business in Hollywood, California. It was a storefront and an office. He sent coupon salespeople to go door-to-door and offer an 8x10 family photograph for one dollar. Perhaps you or your parents did this at one time or another.

A photographer would follow up in a few days and take the pictures of the family. The session included a family portrait, a picture of the mom and dad, and a photo of the kids by themselves. This left plenty of proofs to show to Mom and Dad later. I would make an appointment and come to their home and show them the proofs of the photos. It was my job to sell them more! This was a piece of cake!

First, they would pick the family photo (8x10) that they received for the dollar. Then I would show them the rest of the photos that were taken of the kids by themselves and the ones of the mom and dad together. Of course, I developed my own presentation that I would use for the success of the sale, and it included **asking for the order and not talking**. I would ask which ones they wanted. Sometimes they would just pick, and sometimes they would tell me, "No, I just wanted the 8x10 that came with the promotion." I would then take the worst of the photos and start to rip them up if they showed no interest in extra photos. After seeing me tear them up, some people would change their mind and order one of the package deals that I made up for them. I could change the packages and offer whatever I wanted, but always anywhere from 30 dollars to 125 dollars. I got paid a very nice commission for making the sale. I had the highest average sales in the company.

Here is why I was so successful.

I love selling. It is the most gratifying job in the world. When you get a YES, it feels better than anything, and I mean anything! All you got to do is follow the six points below.

- Have a sales presentation
- Qualify the buyer
- Show the product
- Ask for the order
- Ask for a referral
- Be relentless

Driving home from work with a few sales under your belt, no matter what it is that you sell, is the greatest feeling in the world. It was even better than sex; I learned as I got older.

As time went by, I developed my sales presentation so anyone could use it. My presentation was aggressive. It was a common-sense approach to reaching the highest level of achievement that anyone could. After a couple of years of selling family photographs for someone else, I decided it was time to do it for myself. Here we go again.

6

Ask for the Order!

I WENT into business for myself. I called it California Portraits. Once again, there was no doubt that I would succeed.

We started the business out of the house. In the beginning, it was just me and the ex-wife, who worked with the crew that sold the coupons and the photographer.

The photographer would shoot the picture's, and a crew would go out and sell the coupons for two dollars. I asked one dollar more than the other companies. I wanted us to be different from the others. I felt one more dollar would not make any difference to the family buying it, and it may encourage them to order more, which of course is the whole idea of the business. The coupon selling crew got to keep the two dollars instead of one dollar, which made them more motivated to work for me and sell more appointments. After all, they were making twice as much money. I found out later that some of them were selling the promotion for as much as five dollars. I didn't care as long as I had the appointments. It was a win-win. I would be the one to go out and sell the additional photographs, and of course I needed a plan: a sales presentation. I continued to work on the presentation and develop it so that in the future it could be used by future salespeople we hired.

As the business expanded, I hired additional people to sell the coupons and additional salespeople to sell the photographs. I hired the salespeople (mostly women) and trained them using my sales presentation for their success. Our crews would go into the same neighborhoods several times a year, and we had the same people buying the photos over and over. I was trained to go into lower-income neighborhoods. Believe it or not, they had money for pictures of their kids. They received a welfare check on the first and the fifteenth of every month. It was our job to take part of it away from them. After all, I was trained and learned to believe that if it wasn't me, someone else would take their money It might as well be me or one of my salespeople. We were giving them something that they loved; they were getting pictures of their family.

People that were well off didn't want us in their homes. They preferred a fancy photography studio. Paying attention to my customer's income and desires came in handy throughout my selling career.

Selling the photos went on for several years and we were doing very well, then came the **next great move.** I opened a storefront photography studio. I called it "Photos Are Us."

We offered the customer an opportunity to bring in the family and receive an 8x10 photograph for only five dollars. After all, Sears and JC Penney were very successful at this. I felt that having a neighborhood studio would be very successful. I rented a location and remodeled it with decorations, stuffed animals, and a cage for toddlers to play in. I purchased all the lighting, cameras, and equipment that would be needed. I advertised in the local paper, sent out flyers, and took out ads on the local radio station. We had a grand opening week, and after the first day almost no one came in. I sat around and waited for the families to walk through the door, or at least call and make an appointment. Not much of that happened. I hated it! It sucked!

We had this very nice photography studio and hardly anyone to take pictures of. Those that did come in thought it was great and the product was terrific. Clients really liked it; just not enough of them.

All my life, I had the opportunity to go out and knock on doors and find my own customers. I found myself waiting for them to come to me, again. What a horror that was!

Photos Are Us stayed open for about 16 months, and for 16 months, I paid rent and other expenses. The bottom line; not enough people came in to have their photos taken. As a result, Photos Are Us was a disaster and did not make it.

Oops! Another big failure. I lost six figures or so.

Time to pick myself up and start over again... NO PROBLEM!

I guess by owning drive-in dairies and photography studios, I was looking for easy money. Guess what. **There is no easy money**. If you want something in this world, you have to go out and take it. It's there just looking for you to ask for the order, and it can be yours. Fortunately, I was still selling the photos door-to-door, and this was paying the bills. This was not the way I wanted to spend the rest of my life.

7

Be Relentless

IN 1979, I was 34 years old. I was looking at the classified pages in the *Los Angeles Times*. In those days, we did not have the internet. We used the newspaper to advertise for employees or to find a job. I answered a few ads and talked to a couple of people on the phone. Nothing clicked. One day, I came across an ad that caught my eye. I called the gentleman, and we talked for a very long time. We both seemed to like each other. I liked what he had to say. He liked what I had to say. We agreed to meet in person at his office in the next few days. His name was Ron Lerner. Ron became a very important person and mentor in my life. One of the things I learned from him was when hiring someone you should **hire within your own image.** This stuck with me throughout my career. I passed it on to others.

Ron and I were very much alike. We both felt like if you work hard enough and work honestly, then the success will follow. He worked for a company for many years and had reached a point that he could not go much higher up the ladder. He wanted to leave the cold of Cleveland, Ohio and move his family to sunny Southern California. He was promised a position of Vice President of Sales in the California division of his company located in Los Angeles.

His company broke my number one rule, **don't make promises that you can't keep.** They gave the job to the CEO's nephew. Lucky for me, Ron decided to move to Los Angeles with his family and start his own company anyway. Sound familiar?

As we continued to talk, he told me about the specialty chemical business and how it worked. I loved everything that he said. Everything was in my control. I had the opportunity to sell hundreds and hundreds of products to any kind of business, including industrial, federal, state, city, transportation, construction, and commercial property management. You get the picture. All I needed to do was knock on the door, show the product, and ask for the order. Every one used these products every day.

The salesperson's job was to go in and see the person that oversaw buying the chemical supplies. I didn't have to wait for someone to come to me. I was in complete control. My destiny was in my ability to get someone to order products that they needed.

I asked Ron if I could do a ride-along. That is when you go out into the field with another salesperson and shadow their work. He agreed and set up a day in the field with an existing salesperson. I met with his salesman at a coffee shop at 8 a.m. While he had breakfast, he talked about the job. Finally, we went out and made sales calls to his customers. I quickly realized that I could not only do this job, but that I could do it better than him. One thing that I would do is start my day at 7 a.m. I would have my coffee and donut in the car on the way to my first call of the day. Later I would stop and bring a dozen donuts to the first customer of the day and insisted that salespeople in the future do the same.

The greatest step of my life and in my career was entering the specialty chemical business. All the sales jobs and businesses that I have had were just a test. Getting into the chemical industry was a huge step.

Once again, it was not a case of would we succeed, but how fast would we succeed and how large we would become. Every time I added a new salesperson, I told them that I expected their attitude to be the same as mine. After all, **attitude is everything.** If you believe, you will succeed. Just be relentless; never give up!

In the beginning at Alco Products, I was going to continue to sell baby pictures in the evening and weekends to supplement my income. Ron was aware of this and was fine with the arrangement. It did not last very long. Soon I was a full-time specialty chemical salesperson, and I really loved what I was doing. It was the first time in my professional life that I felt like I had found what I was going to do for the rest of my life.

Talk about scared, but like I said, it was all up to me and my ability to make sales. In 1979, I was making around 50 thousand dollars a year selling baby pictures. That was a lot of money in those days. You can see that making the change was a big deal, but I was not concerned. I knew I would succeed. Ron told me that within a few years I would earn 100 thousand a year or more. I said to him that's great, but don't make it a promise.

I was accepting a job that payed me a one thousand dollar a month draw against 30% commission, no auto allowance, no insurance, no expenses. No, nothing, but the promise of an industry that would provide for me and my family for the next 40 years.

No Problem! For those of you that don't know what a draw against commission is, the company loans you the draw money (let's say 500 dollars twice a month). You get paid on the first and the sixteenth of each month. At the end of the month, you see what your total sales are times 30% commission.

Example: You sell 10,000 dollars in sales, at 30% commission. That equals 3,000 dollars in commission.

The company will deduct the draw (advance) of 1,000 dollars you received on the first and sixteenth. You receive the balance of 2,000 dollars around the twentieth of the following month.

My goal in the beginning was to sell 14,000 dollars in sales each month. This would result in a little over 50,000 dollars a year commission. It was a great goal, but I was starting a job with no customer base in a relatively new territory. They had around four customers that they gave to me, and the rest would require cold calling. This meant knocking on doors every day and building a customer base that would provide me with the living that I was accustomed to. I worked the territory every day and sometimes went out in the field at night. I even went out on the weekend if it meant seeing the buyer that I was looking for. No problem, you learn to do what you had to do to get to where you wanted to be. I was relentless!

Scott and Gary, two of my sons, played youth ice hockey. I was a coach. As a family, it was something that we all enjoyed. One of the things that Ron allowed me to do was have the freedom to continue to coach and attend all hockey games and tournaments. Some were local, but most required traveling all over, including many to Canada and back east. One of the fathers on the team coincidently was a specialty chemical salesperson with a different company. After a year, I convinced him that coming to our company was a better opportunity for him and his family. He agreed.

I introduced and turned over many of my accounts to him, and he continued to sell them as well. He built his own customer base and became one of our top salespeople and my future partner. I'm getting way ahead or myself.

My first day on the job, Ron sent his national sales trainer from San Jose, California, to help me with his sales techniques. His name was Dan Hall. Ron knew Dan from their old company they both worked for in the past, Ron in Cleveland and Dan in California. I picked Dan up at the Burbank airport and off we went to start my new career. He was the meanest, toughest, hard core, high pressure sales-person I have ever seen. He made customers sweat and would not take NO for an answer. One of the first calls we made was to a movie studio in the Burbank area. Dan got us in front of the person that was in charge of buying chemical maintenance supplies. He showed him a few products and went back to his office. He was a suit and tie person (not really who we want to see). Dan would not take no for an answer, and the man called security. They escorted us off the property. By early afternoon that first day, I drove Dan back to Burbank airport, explaining that I could not sell his way and that I would succeed selling on my own. I did say to him that I would use some of his tactics. I called the office and told Ron what I did. He was speechless.

By then, it was late in the afternoon, and I decided to make a cold call on my own near the Burbank Airport. I went to a company that manufactured cement and plaster products. I wanted to get my first call over with. I had no idea what I was doing, but I knew the demonstration of the hand cleaner and the degreaser. I showed the buyer how the products worked by demonstrating the product, like I was trained. I sold Jose (the buyer) a small amount of both prod-ucts and went home feeling like a million dollars. Jose and the cement company became a long-time customer and ordered many products, many times over the years. I also learned that you will not make the sale in this business unless you **make the product demonstration every time**.

What I really needed was a better plan. A better sales presentation that would work for me. A sales presentation that was more in tune with my buyer. It had to be different than what Dan or Ron showed me, but I still wanted to use some of their methods. I needed something that was developed for the blue-collar customer of 1979.

Within months, I developed a bit softer sales presentation that I felt would work well for me and others. It was a 9-point psychological sales presentation directed at the blue-collar worker. The blue-collar worker is the decision maker. This sales presentation would not work on the owner of the company, or the suit and tie guy, or the purchasing agent. In fact, these were the last people that I wanted to see. You had to have the ability to sell all three of these people, but 90% of the time you talked to the blue-collar worker. I called our targeted buyer Archie Bunker.

I taught this presentation or a version of it for the next 35 years to all our sales employees. We worked this plan and reworked it many times until it came to me without even thinking. Of course, over the years, we re-visited it because times and people change, and we had to adjust.

After several months on my own in the field, I discovered a product that Alco Products had in their line called Cover Up. I felt it had different uses than what they were marketing it for. It was an aerosol product that was labeled to cover up graffiti. I thought outside the box, and I got an idea. I took a can into the field and used it for what I thought was a new, unique and different use. I discovered that it was not just a paint cover-up; it contained very strong stain blockers and sealing agents. With just one coat of spray, even red paint would not bleed through. I thought that we should be selling it as a ceiling tile and acoustical ceiling water stain remover. My customers loved it and wanted to buy it on the spot. I told them that we were in the early stages of developing it, and we would have it for sale soon. "*New, different, and unique*" became the theme of my companies in the future. We would tell our customers that the product is, "New, different, and unique," and it was something that they had never seen before and had to have.

I went back to the office and told Ron what we needed to do. I told him that Cover Up needed a new name because I had found another use for it. He called it Acoustical Ceiling Spray-White or ACS-W. All commercial buildings have ceiling tiles; they get water stains all the time. All commercial buildings have blown-on acoustical ceilings, and they also get water stains. ACS-W was the answer to sprucing up their buildings and eliminating those water stains.

Before ACS-W, the customers would have to take the time to take down the stained tiles, cut the new tile, and piece them together. Then they would have to put the new tile back into the ceiling. This took a lot of time and expense. Simply spray ACS-W on the water-stained tile, and it would cover up the stain to the point that looked like it was brand new. Wow! In twenty seconds or so and for about 25 cents, they could fix the tile and move on to something more important. Of course, I had to come up with a plan and a product demonstration to show to the customers on how to use it as well as ACS's features and benefits. We would then make the sales presentation to close the sale, which of course meant you had to ask for the order. Our goal was the make the client's job easier by using our product line. This product was easy to sell, and all we had to do was demo it and ask for the order.

All ceiling tiles and sprayed-on plastered acoustic ceilings begin to turn from white to off-white from age or dirt coming out of the air vent. Cigarette smoke also changes the ceilings from white to off-white. We came out with ACS in off-white or ACW-OW. In just a few years, both shades of this one product helped change this company from a five-salesperson sales team to a twenty-five-person sales team. I made about 50,000 dollars in commissions the first year from the ACS-W and OW product. Not to mention what the company made from it in the years to come. This was one of the products through the years that I realized had potential to perform other jobs for our customers. All we did was rename and re-label. I will tell you about others later.

8

Sales is Interesting and Fun

OVER THE YEARS, I made many sales calls to all kinds of different places. I have been on aircraft carriers and warships at both the San Diego and Norfolk, Virginia Navy bases. I sold product at Arlington cemetery. I sold product to Lockheed Aircraft Company and got to see the stealth bomber in Palmdale, California, years before the public saw it. I sold to colleges, towns, and cities all over the country. I sold to oil well production drillers in Texas and Oklahoma just to name a few. Boy, what fun! What a great job! We can sell something to anyone.

After only a year and a half or so in the field, Alco promoted me to sales manager. My responsibilities were to work with the existing sales team and hire new salespeople. I was paid a small salary plus overrides from the rest of the salespeople. I did continue to sell to some of my best clients that paid me commissions. The rest of my customers I handed off to Rob and other salespeople.

After my promotion to sales manager, Ron ran an ad in the *Los Angeles Times* looking for a salesman. He hired four people, and I got to sit in on the interviews. Ron's philosophy was that if you threw enough shit on the wall, some of it was going to stick. This was one thing that we disagreed on. The four new recruits were to start their classroom training at a local Holiday Inn on Ventura Blvd in Woodland Hills. The following Monday morning at 7:30 a.m., two showed up on time and two were a few minutes late. Around 2 p.m. and after observing the two late candidates, it seemed to me that they were not all that interested and were not part of the training. I decided to terminate both. I thanked them for their time, told them that their career with Alco Products was over, and sent them home. Ron looked at me and said nothing. Later that evening he called me at home and said to me, "Good job today. I have never been more certain that you are the right man for this job." I was happy that he backed me on my decision, especially since I was only on the sales managers job a few weeks.

What is the job of a sales manager?

I really didn't know. I had no formal training and no managing experience. I just figured that I would wing it and just be fair, consistent, and respect my salespeople. Most of all, I would always try to be supportive. Wishful thinking. Sometimes people need their ass kicked as well. The company only had a few salespeople at this time, and I thought I would go out and work with them in the field and see if I could help them in any way with ideas or tips to improve their sales. They were all veteran salesmen that were not excited about any advice or help from me, unless I was going to go out and cold call with them.

I learned fast that when I went out with them, made sales, and opened new accounts, they loved me. If we blanked (had no sales that day) they wondered why I was there. I was only worth cold calling and getting the new customers.

The day I became a sales manager I sat down and wrote something, framed it, and put it on my desk in the small office that Ron gave me. It is still in the original frame and sits next to me now on a bookshelf. It says…

"Remember All problems, no matter how small they may seem are big problems to the person asking or they never would have been mentioned in the first place."

S.C. 1976

9

Building a Sales Team

ALCO PRODUCTS PUT an ad in the *Phoenix Republic* news-paper advertising a need for an outside salesperson. After talking to many people on the phone, I set up six or eight appointments with applicants to meet in Phoenix the next week. I flew to Phoenix the night before my interviews and called all of them confirming our appointments. Of course, I told them that I was very excited to meet with them in person and made them feel like they were the very best of all the candidates. As opposed to the *throw shit till it sticks strategy*, my strategy was to hire the right person for the job. I met with all the applicants the next day and came home without a new salesperson. Ron asked me what happened. I told him I didn't hire anyone. He then told me how much money it cost between the ad in the paper, flight, hotel costs, and my time. I agreed with him, but I said if I don't find the right person, I am not going to hire him just to hire some-one. It cost a lot less not to hire the wrong people than to hire someone and spend months on them, only to later find that this was not the sales job for them.

A few weeks later, I went back to Phoenix and hired my

first salesperson. Let's call him Bob. I wanted him to be great, after all he was to be my first sales rep. Now for the hard part; training him. Bob did remind me of me. Remember, you want to **hire within your own image.** Bob's background was in outside sales selling office machines. He had to learn a canned pitch or a sales presentation that did not allow him to deviate one bit. This is exactly what I wanted if I was going to have him sell our products successfully. I will never forget that he told me that the job was going to be a piece of cake. We called him Cakewalk the entire time that he worked with us–four years. Don't misunderstand me, I wanted all salespeople to stay within the confines of our sales presentation, to adapt it to their personalities, and then have fun with the sale. So long as they stayed within the steps that were established in the sales presentation. At that time, it was a **9-step sales presentation.** Cakewalk turned out to be relentless!

The next week I flew to Phoenix to work with Bob. It was his first week on the job and my plan was to work with him the first three days. I would do most of the selling, using the sales presentation. Whatever was sold would be a sale in Bob's column, meaning he was paid a commission on the sale and the client became his forever. The first morning I did everything, and he just watched and listened. When we got back to the car, we would go over the sales call and talk about everything that was said and done. I would explain why I did something or said something. That afternoon I had Bob do step 1 & 2 of the sale. He was able to do the steps like a seasoned pro. He was a bit clumsy, but he enthusiastically jumped in and did his thing. Bob was like a robot. He stayed right with the presentation and did not deviate one single word. I was excited. I knew right away he was going to do well.

10

The Nine Point Sales Presentation

1. **Detective Work:**

Enter through the back door. Look for drums (barrels) or boxes that contain supplies that the customer has ordered previously. Look at the shipping documents on the boxes or drums; it will list the department that ordered the product and name the person that ordered it. Ask someone where you can find the person whose name appears on the labels. Now that you have his name, find out where his office or shop is located. Look for a worker in a uniform that represents the company. Ask him anything he would rather spend time on other than work. Walk straight forward and look straight ahead and act as if you belong there.

2. **Get Alone with the buyer:**

When you reach the buyer, introduce yourself only by name and ask if you can go to their office. Do not let them talk; just walk towards their office; they will follow you. You don't want to do business with them in the hallway or in a place where their subordinates are around. They will follow you to their office or shop. It's always best to be alone with them.

3. **Warm Up**:

Look around the room and observe pictures of family, sports, etc. Make small talk, and ask them questions. "Is that your son playing football?" Try to get them into a short conversation. Remember no matter what, agree with them.

4. Product:

You have pre-determined a few products that they would like to see, if not switch to a product that would take care of a problem. You have been trained to notice problems while you were walking to their shop. Maybe in the parking lot you saw some oil stains, or you noticed that the bumpers in the parking lot were stained with rust. Or maybe you saw water stains on the ceiling tiles; you know what to show them for that. Take him out to the parking lot and show them your degreaser and rust stain remover. Walk to the parking lot and they will follow. If you don't believe me, try it at home with a friend. Remember: **A presentation without a demonstration is just conversation.**

5. Premium:

Explain to the customer that this month you are having a special incentive to new customers. This is a thank you for your business and your way of saying thank you. A gift card, (Visa, Walmart, or gas card). Again, this is a thank you for the order. Most companies do this. Banks give you something for opening up a new account. Visa or American Express always give something for getting their credit card. You are doing the same thing. Always thank your customer for the business.

6. Close:

Wait for a buying sign, maybe something like, "When will the product arrive?" Or, "How do you ship it, UPS or Fed X?" Or ask them how they want it shipped and when they would like it to arrive. Write it up! Do not talk. Put the order in front of them. Remember **the first one that talks loses.**

7. Pre-Premium and Pre-Product:

Say to your customer, "Mr. customer next month when I stop by, I am going to drop off a gas card for you to use in that big truck that you drive. I am also going to show you a new product that will repair your stained ceiling tiles that you have all around your building. I am talking about a new product that only we have. **It's new, different and unique."**

8. Thank You and Set up next appointment.

Try saying, "What's best for you, morning or afternoon? Once again thanks and I will see you in the morning of the 18th of next month? I'll bring the donuts, and maybe you can have a few of your people here then."

9. Referral:

Ask, "One more thing, is there anyone in the world that you can refer me to that may have need for our products?"

———

EVERY SALESPERSON WAS GIVEN EXTENSIVE SALES TRAINING IN the field, classroom, and on the phone with either me, their manager, or both. In the classroom we videotaped their sales presentation, and then we would critique their performance. There is nothing like seeing yourself in person. Seeing yourself on video is very effective and intense. Most people said that it was the best training tool we ever used. We agreed. It made the difference in our success over the years. When we told them that they were going to be on video, most of them were scared stiff and didn't want to do it. Most were very nervous, but we insisted that they do it. After they did it once, we would erase it and have them do it again. They were twice as good the second time, and we ended up having a lot of fun with it.

There were many ways that the presentation could be done by the salesperson. All the steps of the presentation could be done in a different sequence, but all steps had to be done. This gave them the best chance of closing the sale. Remember, we had set this up so that the salesperson treated it as a cold call. If the salesperson got a sale, it was 1 to 0 in favor of us. Now that we had the first sale, we were on the way to making a new customer. Our goal was to have a **customer for a lifetime.**

One of the most important reminders that we told our sales team was, **"Be positive and be honest at all times."** Next time you see them, the element of surprise is over. They now know who you are and what you're selling. You must stick to the presentation and SELL, SELL, SELL.

It's not until you have sold them at least three times that you get the honor of calling them your customer. Then your goal will be to have him or her become your customer for a lifetime.

Often, I would see salespeople think that after one or two sales that the customer was their friend and they would skip parts of the sales presentation and wonder why the customer stopped ordering. This happened all the time to most salespeople. A salesperson would ask one of us, "What happened? I can't sell anymore. My customers have stopped ordering."

We would reply, "Tell me about your sales call from the time you got out of the car to when you left him. Explain your visit and what you did." It was usually an easy adjustment, so long as they were honest with us. The most common issue was with cutting corners and not going through the complete presentation. Some thought that the customer did not need all the parts of the presentation. Our advice was to not cross the line and get too friendly. Keep it friendly, but it is business. They are not your customer, yet. If the sales associate took our advice, they learned a valuable lesson, and soon they were selling again.

11

Objections and How to Handle Them

Buyers are liars.

SOME CUSTOMERS WANT to see how many salespeople they can get rid of in a day. I had one customer tell me it was fun to get rid of salespeople; he made it a game. However, if you believe that he and his company have the potential to be a great customer one day, then demonstrate to them the products that can make their job easier and that the products will save their department time and money. It is worth the extra sales calls. You are not going to sell everyone the first time that you call on them. It just doesn't happen! You want to make them a **customer for a lifetime.**

One of the most important things that I can tell you is to remember to **always agree, agree, agree, and then once again AGREE with them.** The customer will have objections, and no matter what they are you must agree, smile, and say, "Yes. I understand why you feel this way," and then move forward to **answering their objections.**

"Yes. Customer, (you are agreeing). What if I were able to ship the product now? After all, you did say you could use it now, and I will bill it for you next month." Now be quiet and let him or her respond. If that works, great! But if he says that would be great, but it's still too much money to spend this month, I have to stay within my budget. Your answer should be, "OK, I understand. (Your agreeing, with your head bobbing up and down) And what we should do is split the billing for the next two months, half this month and half next month. OK?" Again, be quiet.

You were going to put him on your 60-75-day cycle to see again anyway, so by the time you get back he is ready to order again.

These and many other objections were covered at our rooking meetings and sometimes at sales meetings. We would spend a great deal of time on objections.

If a salesperson does not agree with the customers when they object, he or she may end up sparring or arguing, and guess what, **you lose.** After all, you're nothing but a lowly salesperson.

Agree, Agree, and Agree, and smile, and move on. This tactic saved my ass thousands of times.

If you do lose and don't get a sale, it's not the end of the world. Move on to the next call. As the **Yes Company,** we insisted that you always agree, agree, and agree.

Other objections you might encounter include the following:

Your price is too high!

Sometimes your customer is going to say, "Well, your price is a little high." Different prospects are going to give us this objection in different ways.

Sometime the customer is going to say, "THAT PRICE IS RIDICULOUS!" Now that's strong, isn't it? When you get these objections with a different tone of voice, you really do have a different objection, and you don't handle it the same way. To the client that says, "THAT PRICE IS RIDICULOUS!" You LOWER your voice, look them right straight in the eye, and ask, "My price is ridiculous?" You will need to practice this several times.

What you have done is move the objection back to the customer's side of the table. Now the customer has to defend his statement, versus you justifying your price. This will require for you not to talk. First one to talk loses. "You know, Customer, many years ago, our company made a basic decision. We decided it would be easier to explain the price one time then to have to justify the quality of our products forever. I'll bet that you're glad that we made that decision, aren't you?"

I'm too busy to talk to you.

"Customer, just as you believe in the value of your time, I believe in the value of our products. I know that our product is going to make your job easier and save you time and labor."

"If you saw a 100-dollar bill laying on the sidewalk, would you have the time to pick it up?"

"If I can't interest you in three minutes or fewer I promise that I will go away and never come back.

We have been buying from XYZ company for over 15 years.

"I understand how safe you feel about a relationship that

goes back for 15 years. I have customers that feel the same way about me as you do them. I saw your eyes light up when you looked at our product demonstration, and you know that XYZ company doesn't have this product. Besides, I am not here to take away their business. I'm here to add to it."

"Actually, we have several products that the competition does not have. They are a great company, and I hear that their salesperson is also very good at what he does."

We tried something like that, but it didn't work.

"What happened? Tell me what happened, so that I can understand and show you the difference between ours and theirs?"

"I am sorry that you had a bad experience. I know how you feel. I have been disappointed with many purchases myself. I can assure you that our product is used by many customers like yourself, and they are very satisfied. Besides, our products are guaranteed to perform to your liking. If they don't work to your satisfaction, we will take it back and exchange it for something else, no questions asked. One more thing, comparing our products of today with what that other company sold you years ago is like comparing a Model T to Mercedes."

I need to talk to my boss.

"If it's a question of showing him the product, let's go see him together, right now. I can help you with any of his questions. Be sure to introduce me as Steve and tell him you really like the product and have a place to use it right now."

"When I first met you, I asked you if you were the

person that does the buying for maintenance. You said yes. Did you lie to me?"

———

THE POWER OF SELLING AND NEGOTIATING ARE ONE IN THE same.

"Everything that you will ever want in life is already owned or controlled by someone else, Therefore, everything you will ever want will have to be negotiated for."

Roger Dawson

How many are you are college grads? When you went to school, how much time was spent negotiating? I bet zero!

I once attended a Roger Dawson seminar, and then I read his book, *Secrets of Power Negotiating.* He was a leading authority in the art of negotiating. Most of what I am writing in this chapter came from his wisdom, and I added parts that worked for me and I think made the negotiation flow better with the result that we wanted.

I believe, negotiating and covering objections are very close to being the same thing when closing a sale. Here are a few different negotiating techniques that I have used over the years, and they are simple for you to learn.

There are three stages of negotiating or making a sale.

1. What exactly do they want, or what do they get out of it? (What's in it for them?)
2. What exactly you or your product can and will do for them. Find out all you can about the other side. Don't assume any information. Ask and get all the information you can. Find out who they buy from, what they buy, and why they use it and where. Even find out the dilution ratios. Know how much they pay for it. Also find out all that you can about the salesperson and company that they are ordering from. There may be some predictable responses, but you must ask the questions to get the answer. **Reach for a compromise.**
3. Your goal is to find value for both of you. This way you both will end up with a win-win solution. People don't always want the same things. What's important to one person is not necessarily important to the other. You must find out what his biggest issue is; exactly what does he want? That does not mean price. Maybe he is simply looking for free bottles and sprayers, free freight, different packaging, or terms. It may be that he is looking for a comfortable relationship with his salesperson. Remember, your goal is to end up with a win-win solution that you both benefit from.

The art of negotiating is to end up where both parties feel as if they have won. I was involved with being part of a deal where the client wanted, needed, our products so that him and his crew could use them but could not get approval from his boss. As I saw it, it needed to be his boss's idea as he wanted the credit of the deal to look good in front of his boss. This was not as difficult as you may think to get the result, so that it looked like they both won. I made an appointment to see my client's boss with his permission as I did not want it to look as I was going behind his back. I met with my client's boss and explained how the products would make his team's job go faster and be more efficient, saving the company time and money. He agreed, after seeing it from this side of the table. He agreed to let my customer make the purchase, and he took the credit for the products that ended up working and saving time and money for the department. We ended up with a win-win situation, both of them felt good and I got the sale. We reached for and obtained a compromise.

So you see. That is a win-win solution that can be reached when you understand people don't always want the same things. Being a good negotiator is not a matter of getting what you want, but it is a concern for the other side to get what they want as well.

Sometimes I worry about the lack of negotiating that some salespeople have. Our goal is to get people to say YES!

Yes, happens to be my favorite word. We even called our company *The Yes Company*. When we hear that magical word, some great things happen.

The next time you put your order book in front of your client and he says, "That's the most outrageous proposition I have ever heard," you need to think about the interesting place you are in to start negotiating.

Here's another example that will help you understand.

Think of yourself as the mayor of a small town, and it's your job to do the negotiating. Let's remember these three stages.

Stage #1: get information, get all the information that you can.

Stage #2: diffuse the situation (calm him down, say yes, and agree with him).

Stage #3: reach for compromise.

TAKE IT OUT

One day, we had a customer call in. He had a problem and was irate. He first spoke to our receptionist, and the issue did not get resolved. He then spoke with our shipping manager, and it still did not get resolved. Finally, the call got to me. Within five minutes, we went over the three stages. We had a solution and a plan. It was very simple.

I had to find out exactly what he wanted, and I asked questions. It turned out a product within a larger order did not do the job that the salesperson said it would. As a result, he wanted to send the entire order back. It was around one thousand dollars, (that's the part I didn't want to hear). However, the customer needed to get all of his frustration off his chest. I agreed with his irritation, and I said yes, I understood him.

I told the customer, "Don't worry, I will take care of it, we will both be happy. My primary concern is that you are satisfied. I will have the salesperson call you back and take care of it right away. I promise you will hear from her today." I spoke to the salesperson within the next half hour and explained to her exactly what I wanted her to do. "Call your customer back and tell him, not to worry, that you will take care of it, and you will be in to see him first thing tomorrow morning. Hang up the phone before he has a chance to talk."

Here is what we have done. We both ensured the customer will be taken care of, we defused the situation, and then re-assured the client. He thinks that you are great. He will cool off overnight and be happy and non-hostile in the morning.

The next morning the salesperson went to see the customer. She agreed and told him, "You are right! I made a mistake by recommending the wrong product for that application." She apologized. We did not have to take anything back, we did exchange the incorrect product and replace it with the correct product that cost a little more. We did not charge the customer. The three stages of a successful negotiation resulted in a win-win solution.

Techniques in Negotiation

There are several techniques in the art of negotiating, some include the following:

1. The classic trade off technique.
2. Good guy/Bad guy.
3. Feel-Felt-Found.
4. Dumb & Dumber.
5. Call girl.
6. Nibbling.
7. Higher authority.

8. Vice Technique.

1. TRADE OFF TECHNIQUE

A while ago, I checked into a hotel in Dallas, Texas. I decided to see what I could do to negotiate the price of my hotel room. At the Dallas Airport Hilton, the rooms went from 165 dollars to 225 dollars per night. Within ten minutes, I was able to receive a reduced price for the room to 70 dollars using this classic trade off technique.

When I arrived at the registration desk, the clerk told me he had only a twin-size room. If they only had a king-size room, I would have complained about that as well. I said I was sorry. I explained that I had the reservation for weeks and will not accept a twin-size room. After several minutes, the manager was brought out. He explained to me that they had 500 rooms in the hotel, and 490 were already occupied. Only 10 were available and that I would have to settle for a twin-size room.

I used the tradeoff technique. I said, "Well I might be willing to settle for a twin room, but if I do that for you, what are you going to do for me?" I paused and waited for their response. I thought maybe they were going to offer me a free breakfast or some such thing, but to my amazement the manager replied, "Mr. Cina, I might be able to adjust the price. What do you think about 70 dollars?"

I replied, "That would be fine." Before he handed over the keys to the room, he said, "Let me see if there is anything else I can do for you." He picked up the phone and called maintenance and asked if a certain room was finished being remodeled and ready for occupancy. The person on the other end of the phone said something to the manager.

He put the phone down and handed me the keys to the 500 dollars per night presidential suite for 70 bucks.

Remember, the most important thing for you to say is, "If I do that for you, what are you going to do for me?" And then shut up. The first one to talk loses. When you get into these situations, I want you to gain the experience. Have fun and practice.

2. Good Guy/Bad Guy

I am sure that you all have seen the classic good-guy/bad-guy in the movies or on TV. You know when the suspect is brought into the police station for interrogation. The first detective screams and yells at the suspect and threatens with all kinds of things they are going to do to their family. Then mysteriously he is called away to take a phone call, and the second detective comes in while the first detective is away. He is quite sincere, warm, and he comes off as the nicest guy that ever lived. He sits down, makes friends with the suspect, gives him a cigarette and says, "Listen kid, it's not all that bad! I've kind of taken a liken to you, and I know the ropes and how things work round here. So why don't you see what I can do for you with them." That's good-guy/ bad-guy.

It's kind of like Dan Hall or your sales manager making your poor customer sweat. Then he excuses himself by telling the customer that he just received a call from the office and has to call in right away. The sales representative then steps in and says to the customer, "I'm really sorry. I will never bring him back in here again. I promise he's just trying to win a bet. He said he could sell you with high-pressure tactics, and I said never. Anyway, he's gone now, can you help me out?"

Good-guy/bad-guy works very effectively even when the other guy knows what you are doing. It is the tactic that President Carter and Ronald Reagan used when they got the American hostages released from the Ayatollah of Iran. That was the year Carter lost the election to Reagan. He was very anxious to do something about the hostage situation with Iranians before he left the White House. So, they played good-guy/ bad-guy with the Ayatollah. Carter started by telling Ayatollah, "Look, if I were you, I'd settle this now with me before Reagan takes over the presidency. You don't want to take a chance with those guys in January. Reagan is a former cowboy actor. The vice president is the head of the CIA (George Bush), and the secretary of state (Alexander Hague) headed up America's armed forces. There is no telling what they might do to your country when they get in power."

Reagan played along with the scheme and said, "If I were you, I would settle with Carter. He is a nice guy. I guarantee you will not like what I have to say about it when I get in the White House." It worked. After 444 days, the 52 American hostages were released on January 20, 1981. It was the same day President Reagan took the oath of office.

These tactics work, even when the other side knows what you are doing.

3. FEEL-FELT-FOUND

Whatever people say to you always agree, don't argue. In response to any proposal that you may make to them, just agree. Most people become defensive and argumentative. Agreeing with them diffuses their competitive feelings. When your client disagrees or objects, just smile and say, "Yes, Mr. or Mrs. Customer. I understand and agree with you." If you disagree, argue, or try to persuade them out of their feelings, it just won't work. Turn it around with the *Feel/Felt/Found Formula.*

For instance, you might say, "Oh yes! I understand exactly how you **FEEL** about this. Many of my customers **FELT** the same way [that's feel and felt], but after you bring in our product, and start using it, you will feel differently."

Show your customer the solution by adding the found. "However, now that we have taken a closer look at the situation and really examined all of our customer's needs, we have always **FOUND** that this is the best way for our customers to go." FEEL-FELT-FOUND. Agree with them and gradually turn them around.

4. DUMB AND DUMBER TECHNIQUE

They say that sophistication breeds competition. Try acting a little dumb, and you will see that it will go a long way to get the yes you are looking for. Do you remember detective Colombo? He was the TV detective with the long overcoat and the old, junkie, brown car. He actually had some of his suspects helping him solve cases against themselves. How smart was that? He was just acting dumb. When I first went in the chemical business as a salesperson, I acted as if it was my first day on the job for the first six months on the job. I find that people will be more receptive to a *newbie*. Most people like to help the new guy. It's kind of like rooting for the underdog. We all like to see them win. That's dumb and dumber technique.

5. CALL GIRL TECHNIQUE

If you do something for your customer, that is above and

beyond the call of duty, the value of the service disappears rapidly after the performance. Maybe you picked a product at the warehouse and delivered it to your customer because he needed right away. Or maybe you needed to go out into the field to show his workers exactly how to use it. Getting yourself dirty goes a long way in the customer service department. Special treatment has great immediate value. Don't be afraid to say to the customer, "I could really use another order today. I did this for you so what are you going to do for me?" Reminding the customer of the favor you did previously, just does not have the same value as asking for the order before you did the work.

Recently, I had to call a plumber to my house. Plumbers always quote the price before they do the work. His price was 125 dollars, and I said, "OK." Five minutes later, he was done and wanted his money. I said to him, "Now, wait just a dawg gone minute. I'm the owner of my own chemical company. I don't even make that much money." It didn't seem like much money before, however after five minutes of work it certainly seemed like a lot. The service was done, and the money for the job was asked for immediately after. That's the call girl technique.

6. Nibbling Technique

Get a little more after all has been agreed on. Car dealers do this all the time. You have made up your mind that you are going to buy a car. The salesman then gets you into the room and starts nibbling. He or she adds on the little expensive extras that have a great deal of profit for them. You may kind of do the same thing by selling one product and adding on another.

I remember on one occasion that I promoted a salesperson to the management team. We had negotiated a contract. We agreed on everything that we needed to agree on, and it was finished. Two hours later, she called me and wanted to nibble a bit more.

I said, "Now Karen. I know exactly what you are doing, and it won't work." The best counterattack is to let them know that you know what they are doing, and it will end it right there.

7. HIGHER AUTHORITY TECHNIQUE

Higher authority is when the customer says that they have to check with their boss, board member, or committee. This is one of the toughest to overcome.

A young man came in and applied for a salespersons job. His interview did not go very well with me. I told him that I would get back to him later. I said that I had to check with my partners. He asked me, "You will recommend me, won't you?" Apparently, he could see in my eyes that I didn't want a conflict with him. After a very quick moment, I looked at him and said I am going to take the first step into hiring you. I'm going to set up an observation day for you to ride in the field with one of our veteran salespeople.

He caught on that there really were no partners. If a customer says to you, "Let me think it over," you should say, "Let's go over it one more time. I must have missed something, because you didn't indicate to me earlier that you couldn't or weren't willing to make a decision today." You have now eliminated their right to refer to a higher authority.

There are times when a customer will say to you that he does have the authority to order, and at the end he may come back and say that he has to check with his boss.

Appeal to the ego.

"Now, Mr. Customer. Your boss always follows your recommendation for the products that you want to use, right?" Then you shut up. That may end it.

Take them to the boss with you there, and then make sure you tell him what to say. Use words like I want it, I like it, and it will work for us.

8. Vice Technique

The sales associate is making a proposal, and the customer says with one eyebrow up, "You're going to have to do a lot better than that if you expect me to order today." The salesperson should respond, "Exactly how much better would you like me to do?"

This way you can pin him down to being more specific and probably give up less than you may have, had you not answered him this way.

A good example of this technique is the Colin Powell story.

At the time of this story, Colin Powell was the Secretary of State. He told one of his under-secretaries he needed a report regarding Iraq in a few days. The next day the report was sent to Mr. Powell. He waited a day or two and put a note on it that said, "You are going to have to do a lot better than this."

On the next attempt, the under-secretary worked on it a lot harder. A couple of graphs were added, and it was sent back to Powell. Again, Powell returned the report with a note, "You still need to do a lot better than this." This time the young under-secretary really worked hard and felt like he had a masterpiece. He made an appointment to see Secretary Powell in person.

He said, "Mr. Secretary, this is the very best that I can do. I can't do any better."

Mr. Powell responded, "If that's the case, I will read it now."

Secretary Powell was using an old college professors' trick. When they don't have time to correct your papers or they want you to be sure you have done the best you can, the professor will put notes on it for you to re-do it. Has this ever happened to you?

In over 30 something years of business, I bet we used the warrantee less that fifty times because we always asked what the customer expected and wanted.

12

Performance Selling

MAKE your sales presentation contain great sincerity and feeling. Never say anything you don't believe in 100%. People trust people that are like themselves. Talk like your customers; speed up your voice with the fast talker. Slow down your delivery with the slow talker. Match the volume or your customer's speech. A loud, fast-talking voice will not work well with a soft-spoken person, and vice versa. It's not only the words said, but how they are said. It's body language that makes one's sales presentation effective. Use these suggestions and others that you already use in the same way that great actors use scripts. Make these suggestions part of the polished delivery of your sales presentation.

You will need to be both mentally and physically prepared to achieve your goals.

SELF-DISCIPLINE. OUTSIDE SALES ALLOWS YOU TO HAVE THE flexibility of creating your own hours. You must have the self-discipline to get out early and to stay out late, making your last sales presentation late into the afternoon.

Time. A four-letter word. The longer you are on the job the better that you are going to do. Once the customer sees you month after month, the more they will begin to trust you. Each time that you do see them develop the relationship. Be their friend, but always introduce and demonstrate a new product to them.

Make friends with everybody. This includes not only the buyer but everyone that works for or with him or her. Learn everyone's first name and call them by it. Give away the little giveaways to the subordinates; they are the ones that will tell the buyer that they like using your products and that they work well.

Take the time to learn and know your customers. Learn their birthdays, anniversaries, both on the job and at home. Learn their kids' names and the name of their wife or girlfriend/boyfriend. Find out what sports their kids' play, and most of all, get them to talk about themselves or the family. Let them talk; do not interrupt. Your job is to listen and record it in your computer or on their customer card.

Never bad mouth the competition. Never say anything bad about another salesperson, company, or its products. The client is ordering from them for the same reasons that you are trying to get him to order from you. Only say nice things about both the company and the salesperson. It's just good business.

Stand behind your company. Never blame anyone else for mistakes, regardless of who was wrong. You take the responsibility and accept the blame yourself. Tell your client that you will make it right. Their relationship is with you, not the shipping, invoicing, or the credit departments. The responsibility of any errors is yours. This will make you look more professional in their eyes. Never set the blame on someone else.

Reach for the stars and the moon. Ask for more than you ever dreamed possible, once in a while you may receive it. If you don't ask, you'll never get it. Make sales calls on accounts that you thought only other salespeople could sell. You may find out that the other rep thought the same thing and didn't have the guts to call on it either. Make the call, shoot for the stars, and don't be afraid.

13

Test Your Skills

Are you in tune with your customers?

USE this self-assessment to see where you are at in your sales skill level and whether you are paying close enough attention to your customers' needs.

- True or False... Your customer almost always returns your phone calls or texts within 24 hours.
- True or False... When you have an appointment, you usually get in to see your customers right on time.
- True or False... New customers tell you what their needs are without resistance or hesitation.
- True or False... Customers frequently glance at their watches during your sales call.
- True or False... You leave most sales calls feeling that you have had a meeting of the minds.
- True or False... You often see your customer

nodding in agreement during your presentation and demonstrations.

- True or False… Customers often interrupt your presentations with comments suggesting that the issues that you are talking about are not their concern.
- True or False… Customers get quiet and hard to read when you get down to business and start talking about the products.
- True or False… Customer often comment "nice presentation" when you leave the meeting.
- True or False… Customers seem to tune in when you talk about the promotional item and the benefits of the product.
- True or False… Customers often tell you more about their specific needs and problems when you are discussing benefits and promotions.
- True or False… You're very comfortable discussing the technical points of the products.
- True or False… You do the selling, but you bring in your manager with the finer points.
- True or False…When you analyze your customers, you pay attention to the technical requirements.
- True or False…You have a top 20% closing rate within the salespeople in your company.
- True or False… You often spend days looking for new prospects, only to find it's difficult to see them for a first appointment and getting the close of the first sale.

HOW TO INTERPRET YOUR ASSESSMENT:

PROFESSIONALISM (Questions 1 thru 4)

When your customer doesn't return your call, keeps you waiting, checks their watch during calls, or seems hesitant to discuss their needs, they may be reacting to a perceived lack of professionalism on your part. Your professionalism speaks for itself. If you look well-groomed and conduct yourself like a responsible and dedicated professional, you will earn the client's trust and business faster. Make a great impression and scrutinize your appearance, sales presentation, and techniques as best as you can.

ANALYZING NEEDS (QUESTIONS 5-7)

Before you can meet a customer's needs, you must understand them. During your presentation, there will be signs of agreement or approval from him or her that will indicate what you are saying is on target. Check to see that the client is paying attention. Either they don't interrupt you at all, or they interrupt you with questions that show their interest. These positive responses are the payoff that you receive when you plan your sales call. Listen carefully, find out what their wants and needs are, and be sure to give it to them.

SELLING BENEFITS (QUESTIONS 8-11)

When you present benefits that appeal to your client, they will respond with questions and interest, rather than silence or little interest. You might hear, "Yeah, come back and see me next time," or, "Leave some literature." Great salespeople know how to communicate benefits in clear, specific terms that a buyer can't resist. You might sell him on a product by promising cleaner, sweet-smelling drains. However, it will sound more enticing when you say, "Most of my customers have found that by using this product in conjunction with an automatic drain feeding machine, you no longer have slow or smelly drains. In fact, 85% of our company's customers have told us that this has solved their drainage problems." Also tell them about a promotion that goes along with the products.

ASKING FOR THE ORDER (Questions 15 and 16)

Getting the order is as easy as asking for it. Assume the sale all the way thru the presentation; write it up and hand the customer the pen and the order pad. Of course, shut up. First to talk will lose. If you have trouble with this, try this, "Mr. Customer, I have addressed all your questions and concerns, and we both agree that this product is right for you. Please trust me with your business today." Again, be quiet!

BE HONEST WITH PEOPLE AND YOUR REPUTATION WILL BE WITH YOU FOREVER

IF YOU ARE A CONSISTENT, HARD SELLING, HARD-WORKING person this will follow you forever, but if you are not a believable salesperson or you are unreliable, this also will follow you. You must be consistent no matter who, no matter how difficult it may be.

Long ago, we witnessed something on television that I never got out of my mind. President Jimmy Carter moved into the white house, and he was carrying his own bags.

From then on, he went downhill. If that had been today, I'm sure that the media would have picked up on this and had an explanation for it, but for me the thought always crept in, "Why does the President of the United States of America carry his own bags?" Somehow seeing the president of the United States of American walk into the white house carrying his own bag makes me think of a sign of weakness. Do you think Iran respected Carter after seeing this? They still had the American hostages and the thought of Reagan taking over the white house made them change their minds and release them the day before Regan took office.

Respect your customers, stay consistent, and care about all people. If you sell with confidence and respect, you will continue to be a powerful salesperson.

ALWAYS ASSUME THE SALE

While going through the presentation, use these subtle statements for assuming the sale.

- I'll send the packing slip to your attention.
- You should receive the product by next week.
- Do you prefer the common carrier or UPS?
- You are smart to order today instead of next week after the price increase.

These statements work smoothly and pass right over a customer's head. You are assuming that every customer is going to buy. You must stay away from asking questions such as, "Where do you want the product sent?" You must assume this and continue with the presentation.

The first lesson taught to every law student is, "Never ask a question without knowing the answer

beforehand." This same lesson applies to selling. You can get yourself into a lot of trouble without knowing the answer. Never ask a question that requires a yes or no answer unless you are absolutely positive that it's a yes!

For example, don't ask, "Do you want me to ship today?" Instead ask, "Do you want me to ship this at once or would you rather I ship it in parts to better fit your budget?"

Get in the habit of using the words "Don't You Agree?"

For instance, "Don't you agree, Mr. customer, that this is the best product to fit your needs? Don't you agree that it works great? Don't you agree that this is something that you can really use?" This is the way that you are asking your clients to agree with you on questions that will get you a definite YES response.

In any business, we should get your customers to take part in the demonstration of your products because you want them to get used to wanting the product by making them a part of the sale; they will feel ownership. Once the client feels ownership, closing becomes a formality. A talented salesperson gets the client involved and then watches for the moment the customer shows approval through body language or the sparkle in the eye.

There are certain words that will assume the sale and certain words that will prevent you from getting the sale. Get into the habit of using the word **WHEN,** instead of **IF.** For example, "*When* you use this product, I can promise that you are going to love it." Instead of saying, *if you use it.* Do you see how **WHEN** is more effective than **IF**? The word **IF** causes the customer to become uncertain. Although you should assume every sale, by no means do. I don't want you to take the customer for granted, even if he is a long-time customer. Never fool yourself that you own your customers because they have been loyal to you. Remember, there is always a new guy lurking, ready to tell the customer that they have something new, different, and something that they have to have. You will have a customer for a lifetime if always treat them as the very first time you sold them. **Don't take them for granted!**

———

Back to Arizona

I was the boss and was making the new rookie salesperson (Bob) do part of the presentation in front of me. I really didn't care how he did it, he just needed to make the effort. If he refused, there was a big problem, and I may want to consider terminating him right there and then. There was no reason to go on; this was a very large potential problem. I remember exactly how he and every rep did their first time that I asked them to participate in our sales process. Can you imagine, your first day on the job, working with a sales manager, and they say, "Ok Joe, it's your turn. You do the first two steps of the presentation on our next call."

Phoenix, Arizona turned out to be a success for us. We ended up with two successful salespeople there. I stayed with Alco Products for five years, and things went well. The company went from around a half million in sales per year to three million when I left.

Which brings me to 1983. I approached Richard at a hockey game and asked if he had any interest in starting our own company. He jumped and said let's look into it. We had no idea how to go about it. I did remember once looking in the yellow pages under *chemicals* and saw a half-page ad that said, "Start your own chemical company."

I called the company and spoke with the owner on the phone. His name was Ken Matney. He invited Richard and me to come to his plant and meet with him. His company was called Orange County Chemical in Anaheim, California. It was about an hour drive from us. We made an appointment. I gave a phony name because I was scared to death that it would get back to Ron that we were talking to Ken. We arrived at the company. It was a large building. We parked down the street and went in. Ken came to the reception area and invited us into his office. We said very little, and he explained that in the past he had helped many people like us get started in their own chemical business. He said that he had over 500 formulations for different cleaning products. His company could make the products that we wanted to put into our line.

Ken then took us in the back to see the manufacturing plant, and holy crap, did it open my eyes. He was making products for all the different companies, including great big competitors. He was making products for Alco Products-the company that we presently worked for.

The way it worked was we would pick the products that we felt would work best for our company and then design the label. That would include writing the text and writing the description. We used the directions of the products on the Orange County Chemical company's label. Once the product was blended, it would be put into different size containers from a quart bottle to a 55-gallon drum. Depending on how many sizes we wanted to offer to our customers. We could order as little as 10 dozen, 10 cases of 4/1 gallon, or one 55-gallon drum of most products. Our plan was to start out small. After all, it was just the two of us selling.

Later, we developed our own formulations to many products. Companies like Ken's would make them for us to our specification's and formulations.

I was dreaming up a plan while we walked around the plant. I planned for my partner to go and sell his old customers from the company that he had before joining Alco Products, and I would start over again 100%. We were both under no-compete contracts with Alco Products, and we planned to abide by that contract. This was the beginning of the plan, and we had a lot to figure out.

By the time we finished our tour and went into Ken's office, we felt comfortable with him and told him our real names and where we came from. Ken also reassured us that he did not talk to other companies about who he did business with, even if asked directly. Ken explained that his company only made liquid bulk products and did not offer aerosol products. He did offer a referral to us that made aerosols called Chemical Packaging from Fort Lauderdale, Florida. They had a warehouse in Ontario, California. Ken was nice enough to give us their number and contact name.

I called Chemical Packaging and spoke to a woman named Diana. She was very nice, and I told her our story. She oversaw the west coast operation, and her husband, Jim, was the sales manager. She invited us in; they were always looking for new customers. We set up an appointment for the next week. Once again, our eyes and minds were blown wide open pretty much the same names on the aerosol cans including Alco Products, the company we worked for now. This was a warehouse, not a manufacturing facility. They received inventory or products from Florida that they called white stock (no labels) in Ontario. They would print our labels and store them there. As we ordered products, they would put our labels on the white stock and ship to us. Again, most of the same competitors we saw at Orange County Chemical were also clients of Chemical Packaging. They had both given us literature of their products and services and price lists. We told them that we would get back to them later.

I loved my job at Alco, and I was earning more than I ever had in my life. I have always had that entrepreneur spirit. I love putting myself out on the line, being responsible for other people and their families, and helping them to succeed as well as succeeding myself. I guess the thought of owning my own specialty chemical company was too much for me to resist. After all, I knew that I would succeed; the only question was at what level I would succeed. I was always sure of myself and my ability to make it no matter what I was doing.

On the last Friday before New Year's 1983, I walked into Ron's office and told him that I won't be back. Richard and I were leaving and starting our own company. I told him that we both were honoring our non-compete agreements that we had with him. After I picked him up off the floor, he wished us well and we remained friends until he passed.

14

Business Owner Mindset

THIS WAS to be the biggest step in my life.

All the sales jobs and business's that I had prior were just practice. It was the big time. No more working just with salespeople or doing the selling by myself. I had to learn about the inside part of business. I had to learn about the shipping, billing, buying, office team personnel, the IRS, the EEOC, taxes, workmen's compensation, and worst of all lawyers. Working with an office and warehouse team was new too. I had to remember to listen and respect them.

Yes, I have a huge ego and I recognize it. I think that I keep it in check most of the time. Getting into the chemical industry on my own was a huge step. Once again, it was not a case of would we succeed, but how fast would we succeed and how big we would grow.

Every time we added a new salesperson, I told them that this is what your attitude needs to be, and the company will do all that is needed in order to help them succeed.

Richard had a friend that had a trucking company in Burbank, California, with a warehouse. He was willing to rent us one thousand square feet of it. We had a fence built around it inside the warehouse to provide a little space for inventory. We also rented an old trailer for our office and set it up in the back of the property.

I had no idea how much was needed to start our company of two. We only wanted to sell our products with our name on them (private label). We started with about 50 products. We needed to design a logo for the company. Then we had to name and describe the product and how it worked on the label. Keeping it simple was the theme; do not make it complicated. This was a huge job, and it took us into the night and weekends for months. As we got some products named, we then sent them to (Ken) Orange County Chemical and (Diana) Chemical Packaging to be filled and labeled.

I was very proud when the first products came in. Of course, our flagship products included Acusta White and Acusta Off White, the ceiling sprays. The most important thing to get across to the customer was that our products were new, different, and unique. We would do the demonstration, and the customers were told that we were the only company that had these products for sale in the industry.

We would go out early in the morning and make sales calls all day, and at the end of the day we would go to the office/warehouse and type, fill, and ship the orders. Some would ship by UPS and some via truck. We would do everything by ourselves. We worked 12 to 14-hour days and on the weekends, no matter what it took.

In the fall of 1983, we heard of a trade show that was being held in Los Angeles at the convention center. I was able to get us passes to the show. Once again, I had no idea what to expect. Holy shit! When we went into the convention center hall, my eyes were as big as hockey pucks. There were hundreds of companies displaying their products.

There were cleaning supply companies. Companies that manufactured greases and lubricants; there were roofing materials like patches and sealers. There were companies that made asphalt materials and repair products. There were companies that made insecticides and weed killers. There were companies that made product for every customer we had and then 100 times more. This was a new world for us, and the future was wide open. I walked through all the different booths for the next three days. We tried to see as many of the exhibitors as we could and introduce ourselves to them.

The International Sanitary Supply Association (ISSA) is the leading trade association for the cleaning industry worldwide. The ISSA Show was held for the first and last time in Los Angeles that year. What a break that we stumbled upon it then; what may have happened? Who knows how long it may have been until we found it, If ever? We signed up with the ISSA and we were members for the next 40 years or so. Each year we would go to the convention, and every year we would add suppliers and new products to our line.

I made friends there that lasted for over 40 years. These were suppliers that we did business with throughout my career.

More Trade Show Talk

It wasn't long before we began showing our products at trade shows. I found a trade show at the Orange County Convention Center in 2006. A company that put together trade shows around the country produced it. They got engineering and maintenance people together to look at exhibitor's products. There were no specialty chemical companies there like ours. I thought, *Fantastic*. I thought we should exhibit our products and see what happens.

This was the first time we paid for a booth and all the extras that went with it: power, carpet, table and chairs. What a rip-off! We did not have an exhibiting booth, but we bought a large canvas backdrop with our name and information printed on it. It was a two-day event. I was there with Dan, and we brought in some of our female salespeople.

People were fighting to get to our booth and see and talk to us about our products. I think that it was really to talk to some of our saleswomen that were doing demonstrations of the products and selling right on the spot. We also were collecting many leads for future sales. We started to do several of these trade shows around the country, including in Boston, Chicago, Orange County, Philadelphia, and others. This went on for about 10 years, and unfortunately, they stopped having them.

This was another example of thinking out of the box once again and doing something different from the competition. Other companies found out that we were exhibiting, and they started to as well. It seemed a tiny little company like us was leading the way in our industry in regards to new ways to do things.

Product lines

I started in the specialty chemical industry with Alco Products in 1979. They had a quality product line. At the time, there was no one that I knew of that sold for less money. Their prices were high!

They offered products to the "end user" of a school district or a city, state, county, all departments, sanitation, department of transportation, literally everyone. Wow, what a business.

While we were developing our product line, we decided from the beginning that we were going to have the best products available to our sales team and customers. Through the years, as the chemistry changed for the better, we would change with it. Sometimes that meant that we would discontinue a product for a new product that was developed with what was I called "New Chemistry." We were selling our products for top dollar, and I would never offer a product that was not the best available.

There were many companies selling for less than us, and their products were inferior. If a customer said why are your products better? We would prove that in the field by doing back-to-back demonstrations in front of the customer. Also, the competition's salespeople were "Order Takers." Ours were trained professional salespeople. There is a difference.

I always reminded them that there will always be someone out there selling something for cheaper! One thing that I knew was you get what you pay for in life, period! That included specialty chemicals.

"We never had to make an excuse for the quality of our products."

15

Sales and Service to our Customers and Sales Team

IT IS essential to provide service to both the customer and the salespeople. Yes, I include both because they are both important parts of our success. As I stated earlier, I was not very patient, and everything needed to get done as soon as it came up. If you are a customer and have a question about an invoice or a product, you appreciate doing business with a company that can answer and take care of your concerns quickly. I wanted both the office team and sales team to be able to answer a question on the spot or as soon as possible. That's why our outside salespeople after one year or so on the job were encouraged to answer customer product or invoice questions immediately. If they couldn't, they had to get back to them within 24 hours or fewer. They had the authority to answer to their clients. Not say, "I have to check with my boss." I hate it when someone says to me, "I have to check with my boss." I wanted our reps to answer a question right there and then as many times as possible. If a customer was willing to buy on the spot, but asked for a better price, our salespeople had many options that they could use in order to get the sale right there and then. The customer loved the fact that their rep could decide on the spot.

The office team was told to answer any question they could or get the question to someone who could answer it immediately. I was available to answer all questions from either the office of the sales team any time of the day or night, and they all knew this.

Another great part of our service in the last 10 years was our website. It was very informative, easy to navigate, and it also had a section that you could learn about our product line, both with lots of information and YouTube product videos. We were told by customers and others that they loved the website and enjoyed using it.

We had fast shipping. After a salesperson put an order into the system, it was pulled and shipped the next day 96% of the time and delivered the day after that. If it was a California, Arizona, Nevada, or Midwest order, it was delivered in three to four days. East coast orders were delivered in five to seven days. If the order came out of the eastern warehouse, they were delivered in two to three days.

Our product line took a back seat to no one else's. We had hundreds and hundreds of products that helped our customers. Everything from janitorial products to water treatment to plumbing and drain maintenance and everything from the floorboards to the top of the roof, and everything in between. If we didn't have it, we would get it for you so long as it was a fair price.

Our products sold themselves. We had a demonstration for just about every product. When we showed it to the customer, it would just about sell itself. Our products performed as stated and if they did not, we had a warranty from day one. As they followed the directions on the label, we were more than happy to take the product back and replace it with something else. NO QUESTIONS ASKED!

I can tell you that over 30 something years I bet we used the warrantee less that fifty times.

16

Finding our New Team

AFTER ABOUT SIX MONTHS, we were selling enough that we felt that we could hire a part-time person in the office. Let's call her Didi. Once again, we got lucky. She knew how to do just about everything, and what she didn't know she learned fast or figured it out. With Didi doing most of the billing, invoicing, answering phones, etc., I had time to think about building a sales force. We still didn't have computers, but they were coming. We did everything by hand.

My brother Joe had been asking for a sales position for a long time, even before we started our own company. Now that we were on our own, I finally said yes. He had no sales experience of any kind. My entire family from my father to brothers and uncles to cousins all were plastering contractors; all of them, except for me. I told Joe that he better be all in, because I did not look at this or anything else as a trial basis. Both of us had to be 100% committed. Joe needed to do what he was taught and make it work his way. He was not to be a robot, but to use his personality and story. He brought with him his experience as a contractor/blue-collar guy like our customers. They related. Joe started with us as our first salesperson and stayed until his retirement after 23 years of full-time service. After that, he kept a handful of lifelong customers and still sells them today part time.

One of the other things that I wanted to bring to the company was an old fashion kind of sales organization. Not corporate America! One that cared about its employees and especially its salespeople, and we were willing to prove it to them by offering extras like high commissions, sales contests, auto allowance, and insurance for their families. We were more than happy to make available to our sales staff whatever they need to be successful and we did. Remember happy wife happy life? We went with happy salespeople, happy company. We became a leader in the industry. It set us apart from all the competition. In fact, over the years to come, others used our techniques as part of their business plan.

When it was time to add more new salesmen to the company, who do you think I hired to train them? Yep, none other than Mr. Dan Hall, my first trainer with Alco Products. Dan started with my brother Joe for a few weeks to get acquainted with our product line and help Joe with his customer base. They both enjoyed it. When Dan wasn't working with Joe, he spent his time in his home area of northern California. Dan opened accounts on his own with the understanding that he would give up his clients and become our full-time national sales manager.

When we were recruiting there were many things that we looked for in the potential salesperson.

The very first thing that I looked for was did they shake my hand hard and look me straight in the eye. If they looked away, this was not a good sign. The next thing I looked at was their shoes. It didn't matter if they were men or women; were their shoes scuffed or shined? If they were scuffed, this meant that they were lazy and did not care about their appearance. If the applicant was male, I looked at how they were dressed. Did they wear a suit or sport coat or no coat at all? If they were female, I also looked at their makeup; was it applied well? I liked bright red lipstick; I felt like red was an aggressive color. We also paid attention if they were on time. Being on time meant being 15 minutes early. If they were late, it was bad, even if they called me and told me that they were running late for our interview. It was not a job buster, but strikes were taken in the final analysis. To me, applying for the job should have been the most important thing going on in their life at that time, and nothing should get in the way of being on time.

I held myself to a high standard, and I made sure they asked good questions. For example, "How long do other people stay with the company? As a salesperson for this company, what is expected of them?" I liked it when they dominated the conversation. I didn't like the question, "How much do you pay?" Of course, we had no problem with answering questions about commissions or benefits, but we wanted a motivated sales team. We were also looking for people that answered our questions with more than a one-word answer.

We were looking for people that came across with a "WE" attitude, not an "I" attitude. I was looking for sheep herders not sheep!

In April 1984, I ran an ad in the Los Angeles area to hire our second salesperson. I would interview and recruit the same way I had at Alco Products. As they say, "If it's not broke, don't fix it." The way I recruited never changed, and I taught all of my managers in the years to come the same way. The calls came in, and I went out to interview them at a local hotel. I set up eight to ten appointments each day, starting early. If they were on time, good. If not, let them wait till there is a break in the schedule. If they had bright shiny shoes, great. I looked for someone within my image. I was putting together a team.

I met a young man from Los Angeles named Juan M. I loved him. He had everything that I was looking for. He accepted the job and later told me the reason that he accepted was because he believed in me and what we were going to accomplish in the future. He stayed a few years and did well. Unfortunately for us, he moved on to a new field. We stayed in touch. Juan is a winner.

In the meantime, we began to hire other salesmen, and some did well, some did not. For those that did not make it, we could now offer to their replacements some accounts that were being sold by the company. This way they had a small base to start their career with. I called this *Building on Bones.*

We then ran an ad in Sacramento, California, in 1987. I went through all the resumes, talked to many of them, and set up appointments to meet them in person. I flew to Sacramento, where I met up with Dan. We did the interviews together and offered the job to four people. They all turned us down. We then interviewed and hired Pastor Bill. Bill was our fifth choice. I loved telling Bill's story, and I did many times over the years at sales meetings. It was good fun, and Bill was just fine with it. Bill is still with it, and it's been 33 years. Bill loved the concept of the premium and used it skillfully. I dubbed Bill the "Apartment King of Sacramento." He never made appointments with his customers; it was not necessary. He would show up at his client's office or security gate and ask to see his customer by name. They would then get the customer on the two-way radio and say, "Bill's here." The customer would say, "Have him meet me at my shop or the office, I will be right there." This is how popular he is with them, no last name and no company name; he was just Bill. Wow, what a great hire, and what a great man Bill is. Hopefully, we will be friends with Bill and his wife Jeannie forever.

I know this because I road with Bill several times in the field. I made it a habit to get around and work in the field with all our salespeople. I think they enjoyed it and it gave us special time together.

Dan and northern California continued to grow. In 1987, we hired Ganine F., and in 1988 Lisa from Walnut Creek, California. Lisa did everything wrong, but when I left 30 years later, she too was still selling for us. Wow!

In 1988, I also hired Jill from Mountain View and Rolfe from Orangeville, California, all on Dan's team.

In 1989, one of my sons, Randy, began to sell on our sales team. After a few years, Randy started to train salespeople. After a bit, he did his own recruiting. He brought Belinda Anderson of Los Angeles, Kathleen O'Conner, Oceanside, California, and Kathy Allen from Woodland Hills. The list goes on and on for the next 20 or so years. Many of these people stayed and did well, and many did not. I am grateful to all of them, because they each helped us get better at our jobs.

As we hired and grew, we introduced our way of selling to all the salespeople. We had them go through the sales presentation from beginning to end on every sales call without exception. Without it, sales calls were a waste of time. Show customers how the product works, why it will work for them, and how much time and money it will save their company. Every sales rep was trained to sell our products this way to start with and not to change a thing. Some failed and others succeeded at whatever level they wanted to. Some made six figures and above. Most or our salespeople in all fields, even ours, seemed to level off to where they were comfortable. Some do continue to grow. They are the ones who never get comfortable and seem to always want more. For those that choose to stop and be comfortable, I never could find a way to change that. So, I embraced their achievements and was happy for them. They were still earning more than the average income, and most importantly they were their own boss with limited supervision. They seemed happy with their situation and I always said give me twenty of them; they are very profitable. Not everyone is a top gun.

17

A Team of Women

WE WERE the first specialty chemical company to hire women salespeople in the industry. I believed this changed the way customers purchased their supplies.

Until this point in my history, I didn't think this was a job for women. Our sales call was pitched to a blue-collar worker, a maintenance man, a nice guy. These were good guys, but maybe a little crude sometimes. Many times, we visited with them in their shops or offices that were in the basement or boiler room of the building and many of them had nude centerfolds on the walls. I wasn't completely comfortable with this situation, but it worked out fine. It was a different time. All our salespeople looked and acted professional. All men had to wear a dress shirt and tie. All women were asked to dress conservatively in skirts just above the knee, and no open tops. It didn't take long for the customers calendars to change from nude centerfolds to race cars. We gave out calendars with race cars as a promotion to customers free of charge.

By this time, The Yes Company had moved out of the trailer and up the street to our first 5,500 square foot building. We thought this was huge, and we were very excited. By this time, I had an assistant, Sally, and all my calls went through her. She was told, way back then, that I didn't want to talk to any females calling in for the job ads. You may not believe this, but it is true.

Most days I still went out in the field to see and sell my own clients. One Monday morning, I was in downtown Los Angeles in skid row calling on a very low-class but semi-large hotel that used many of our products. I stopped at a phone booth across the street from the hotel. There weren't cell phones in these days. I called to let my customer know I was on my way to see him. I looked across the street at another phone booth and saw a young lady in a red dress. She really caught my eye; she was very attractive. I wondered what she was doing in this part of the city. I then went to see my customer. He bought 20 gallons of insecticide and some mal-odor counteract (air freshener). It was almost 1000 dollar's worth of products.

The next day, I was expecting a call and answered the phone myself. There was a woman on the phone with a very high-pitched funny voice and a strong South African accent. She said, "I am applying for a sales position." I was intrigued and let her talk and talk and talk some more. She was controlling the conversation. I was reminded that control was the main ingredient of our sales presentation. We made an appointment to meet in my office the next day.

My appointment arrived on time. I went out front to greet her and HOLY SHIT. I could not believe that I was looking at the girl from the phone booth. Her name was Topaz Summerfield, and she was from Zimbabwe.

I told her that I saw her in Los Angeles at the phone booth and sure enough; it was her. We started the interview, but I knew that moment that she was going to be the first saleswoman at our company. There is no way that any customer would not let her in the door. They would be curious what she was doing there and getting in the door to show your products may be the most difficult part of our, or any, sales presentation. How can you make a sale if you can't get in the door? Advantage Topaz!

She did have some experience in retail sales in a department store. She said that she did well, but she was bored and was looking for someone to give her a chance at outside sales. She wanted a job where she could make a lot of money. I explained that this was all outside sales and the only thing she had to do was make the calls and make the sale. I explained to her that what we did was a numbers game, and if she made enough calls and asked enough people to buy something, someone would say yes. At our company, the office did everything but make the sale. The office would do the billing, shipping, and collecting of money. The salespeople spent 100% of their time in the field making sales. This is what was so attractive to most of the potential salespeople that we interviewed over the years. I explained to her that this was a commission only sales position with a draw of 1000 dollars per month. My feeling was that anyone that would take this job under these circumstances (pay) had to be very sure of themselves and their ability as a salesperson, and they had to have confidence in themselves.

Later we offered salary, auto allowances, insurance benefits, premiums allowances, and more, but now just a small draw and nothing else.

What was impressive to me is that Topaz left her home, family, and friends to start a new life in the United States. What balls did that take? Wow! It told me she had to succeed, and she was very interested in making lots of money. Topaz was money motivated! I also felt that women wanted to succeed in our world. Frankly, I thought they had a small chip on their shoulder and needed to prove that they could succeed in a male-dominated industry.

"Topaz you are hired! We are glad to have you here." Years later, after a trip to South Africa, she brought me a gift. It was a small carved elephant made of a rare African stone called verdite. I still have the elephant on my desk to this day and it reminds me of Topaz Summerfield every day. After she left us, she opened a gallery in Santa Monica that did very well for many years. I spoke to her recently, and she told me she has a home in Idyllwild, California in the mountains and lives part time in Wales, Great Britain with her husband. She says, "I am *Bi-Continental*."

I called Dan and told him that I hired a female salesperson, and boy he could not wait to train a woman. I did remind him that he is always representing our company and to keep it professional. I was also going to help with some of her training. What I suspected came true. From the first week that she started on her own, it was easier for her to get in the door on cold calls than any man. It was a difference maker. However, Topaz and every woman after her better have something good to say about why she was there, in other words they had better know their product line as well as anyone. As a result, much of her hard work and cold calling resulted in many new clients for her and the company. I could not have asked for a better situation. It didn't take long for her to become one of our top salespeople.

Topaz lived in Santa Monica, where there was a group of transplants she hung out with. They were from all over the world, South Africa, England, Scotland, and Ireland. Most of them had similar circumstances. They moved here to America, single, and wanted to make money. Some were interested in interviewing with us. What gutsy and brave women they were.

In the next few months, we hired several of her friends. Jan was from Ireland. She had very little sales experience, but she had confidence in herself, needed money, and could not afford to fail. We hired two Joanne's, both from England, and Jeanne was from South Africa. As hoped, they were all on their way to learning the specialty chemical business and our way of presenting our products. They had great work habits; they were up and out early, and they stayed out till late in the afternoon. If they had a bad day going at noon, they did not go home; they continued making sales calls knowing that it takes one sale to make the day. I always have said about people, **"You can't teach work habits."** Work habits are learned in the home as part as your upbringing. I am sorry to say that many of today's young people are lazy and not willing to put in what it takes to succeed. Many think that they are entitled. Many have come to expect to be given things that we earned in the past. You just can't teach work habits.

By this time, we were hiring women almost exclusively.

One of Topaz's friends was Jeanne S. Jeanne was the friend from Cape Town, South Africa. When I first interviewed her, she was arrogant, pushy, and had the ability to take charge. Of course, I loved all of this. We now had my sons and four or five women working in the greater Los Angeles area, and we thought we would look in the Orange/San Bernardino counties and south to San Diego.

As the first to hire women salespeople in the industry, we had a definite advantage over the competition. We noticed that the competition would bad mouth us and our saleswomen. I always taught, **"Never bad mouth another**

salesperson or a competitor." The client is working with them because they like them, and it will not help you look very good in the client's mind to bad mouth another. Especially when the customer likes our women salesperson.

Up until now, I wasn't convinced that this was a job for women. I was wrong! Our ads would say, "Women are encouraged to apply."

We did still hire men, of course. By this time, Dan had help in Southern California with the teaching and training of new salespeople. Randy was working as a salesperson in Los Angeles and was also recruiting and training. We ran ads in both Orange County and San Diego.

Randy was very good at recruiting; he went to San Diego where he interviewed and hired a young lady named Jessica. She was young and determined to succeed at the job. We always looked for something that we felt set them apart from the others; we wanted something that made them a little different. In Jessica's case, she had a great attitude and high pitched and different voice that the customers were going to remember. It took her some time to catch on, but with Randy's support and help, her sales began to rise, and her customers were very loyal. After a while, Jessica married, and her husband was transferred by his company to the greater Washington D.C. area. Jessica asked if she could stay on with us and of course we said yes. She now had to start over again, and I can't tell you how hard that can be. This would be the second new territory that she would open.

She did well in D.C., starting over again and building a new customer base. Once again, her husband transferred to Valencia, California; coincidently, it was our home base. Jessica again wanted to stay on with us, and we said yes again, of course. This time we did have a few accounts that we could give her, and off she went again to start over. Soon after, she was pregnant, and James was born. Jessica was doing well, but her marriage was ending, and she missed San Diego and wanted to move back. We had another sales-person in San Diego. So again, she needed to start a new customer base and territory. Lucky for her, there were some old customers that were no longer ordering from us, and Jessica was able to get them back. Twenty-three years later, Jessica is still going very strong.

Bringing women into our company turned out to grow our business much faster than I could have dreamed. I think that they are more motivated and much hungrier than others. I got lucky that day in downtown Los Angeles; seeing and then hiring Topaz was the beginning of fantastic growth. Soon after, much of the competition hired women. Soon women were equal to men in sales, not only in our industry but many industries throughout the country.

18

Growing Northern California and Beyond

LOREN WAS IN FRESNO, California, and she wanted to move to the San Jose area in northern California. After she moved, we replaced her with a new person in Fresno. After all, we had many customers in Fresno. Whenever we replaced a salesperson in a territory with a new person, we made sure that the new person learned the sales presentation and cold called the territory every day. They were not allowed to call on the existing customers until we felt that they were ready. If they were taken out to see the existing customers from day one all they would be doing is taking orders; taking orders is not learning how to sell. After a short time, our trainers would introduce them to the customer base that was there for them to service.

Loren moved to the San Jose area and worked with Dan; however, she was experienced and did not need as much training as most people. She was more comfortable working by herself, and we had no problem with it. After several months, she began to developed many new customers.

I ran the newspaper ads in the north, and I did the in-person interviewing of the applicants with Dan. When we decided which applicants we liked for the position, Dan would send them out with an experienced salesperson to do the ride-along. This was not only for us to get feedback from the person they went out with, but this gave the applicant the opportunity to see exactly what the job looked like. We both benefited from the ride-along. Our hiring process was very structured, and we stayed with it regardless of the cost or the time invested in it. Most of the time we would do interviews in a city that we did not have salespeople.

Let's say we were hiring in Oklahoma City. I would have to fly there and get a hotel. I always got a suite, so the interview would be done in the living room portion of the suite with the door open; women found this much more comfortable, and so did I. Then we would have to fly the selected person or people to a city where we did have salespeople so that we could do the ride along. We had two airline flights, two hotel stays, expenses for food and miscellaneous expenses. It all added up, but it was worth every penny. We always said, "If you pay now, you will pay less later."

For the next few years, things continued to go well, and the company continued to grow. We had about seven salespeople in northern California, and Dan had a customer (maintenance man) that wanted a job with us selling our products. I said no for the longest time. He had no sales experience, and I did not think he was for us. He continued to work on Dan for the job, and finally I gave in to Dan's recommendation. His area was in and around the city of San Francisco.

He started selling as a salesperson in San Francisco. Dan and he became quite friendly. He was doing very well as a salesperson and he wanted to be part of our sales management team. After two years, he was promoted to sales manager and worked with Dan in northern California.

A couple of years later he quit us and took Loren, Dan and four of our salespeople with him. They started their own business with no intention of honoring their contracts. I was not very happy. After all, it cost us about 1.2 million dollars in business. I decided to sue them for breaking their contracts. All of them continued to sell our customers.

This was a long process that for me was lots of fun; I kind of enjoyed it. I enjoyed having them come in for depositions and court appearances every day. They were in deposition; they were out of the field, and it cost them money, something they did not have a lot of. Two of the salespeople quit them. I guess the stress of the lawsuit and the uncertainty of their future was not clear.

The lawsuit cost both companies a great deal of money, and more importantly it took my focus away from what I really should have been doing full time. We did get an injunction against all of them that stopped them from calling on some customers for a while. After that, another salesperson they stole also quit. The court ordered all of them to stay out of some customers for good. No one won. They are still in business, and he has made a career of stealing other company's salespeople.

Throughout the years, other people left us to start their own business. Some abided by their contract, and I have nothing but respect for them. Others quit, and I felt that they were not worthy of suing; they just were not a threat to us. In fact, I began to look at it as a compliment. We must have trained them well. Hopefully, everyone that ever worked for me had confidence in themselves. I hope so.

19

Expanding to the Eastern Region

IN MAY 1993, I got a phone call from Don Wellman. He told me that he was a sales manager with another specialty chemical company, a very large company, that had been in business since 1919. He said that he had been there for many years, and that it looked like his time was up. He also said he had two other people that were looking to talk with us.

He and another associate lived and worked in Connecticut, and the third was from Atlanta. He had heard about our reputation, and he wanted to meet with me. I agreed and was on a plane to Hartford the next week.

Don and I met and talked for a long time. He said that his company was terminating most of the veteran management staff and replacing them with younger and cheaper managers. I was skeptical. I thought maybe he was just not doing his job as well these days. There are always two sides to all stories. At the time, we had no one in Atlanta and a couple of reps in the eastern region. There were none in Connecticut. Don had accounts of his own, and the other salesperson, Anne, had an account base of her own. She would leave out of loyalty to Don; he was her manager. I met with Don and Anne and it was decided that they were to join The Yes Company.

Harry was the third person; he lived in Atlanta. I met the next week with him in Atlanta. He was an old-timer with many years of chemical experience. As a matter of fact, I had heard of him prior to our meeting. He had a reputation as an icon in the industry. He invented the premium to the sales presentation, "The Power of the Premium." His sales presentation was used by his company across America. It was a 7-point sales pitch; it was similar to ours, except he was very offensive to the customer. His pitch made the gift the most important part. We offered customer a promotion as a thank you and not a bribe. Back in his day, it was nothing to give a potential customer a television or expensive gifts if the order was large enough. We never were quite that bold, but we did believe in the power of the premium. The company that Harry came from was the most aggressive company in the industry, and Harry was the most aggressive of them all. However, Harry and I agreed that the difference between the way he did sell and the way we sell now was a positive step forward, and he believed he would sell our products our way. He had so much experience that I could not help but want him on our team. He also had knowledge of potential customers in Atlanta and the surrounding towns, and he had his own customers that he had been selling for years.

Dan also new Harry from Atlanta. They worked together for the same company in the past and highly recommended that we hire him.

I thought that by hiring Dave, Anne, and Harry that their former company would file a lawsuit against us. They did. They even had in-house attorneys and lots of experience in this area. We had very little, but we knew that Georgia and Connecticut were "Right to work" states that hopefully would work in our favor. We also knew that this was going to be expensive to fight. I factored in the amount of sales dollars that the three of them would bring in, plus the possible growth of new salespeople from Harry in the south and Don in the Northeast. It was a no brainer for me. Harry successfully trained some new people for us. One of which went on and hired, trained, and developed her own sales team in Texas and the mid-west. We never hired anyone that didn't contact us first, and they were looking to make a change for whatever reason they deemed.

Harry was semi-retired after a few years with us, and he worked for his son-in-law for a while. He and his wife moved to Florida, and I appreciate all he did for our company.

Harry taught me a very interesting theory on work habits. He said to me one day about being sick or not feeling well, "You can stay home and not feel well, and not work, and make no money, or you can get your ass up and go to work and make some money." Like I said, Harry was an old timer, but we loved him.

Don stayed a few years and did well for himself. Anne just recently left due to new ownership.

20

Keep Your Friends Close and Competitors Closer

AFTER THE LAWSUIT, I became friendly with the President and CEO of the company that sued us. They had around 200 salespeople and their sales were about 100 million dollars a year. I think he was very interested in how we could take a company from nothing and build it to where it was. It just was not being done anywhere else. Frankly, I was very interested in how they operated their company. I talked to Harold several times a year, and we started to meet for dinner at the annual ISSA trade show either in Las Vegas or Chicago.

Harold wanted to buy our company. We were never able to put a deal together. Unfortunately, Harold passed away. His son took over the company just as Harold did from his father-in-law when he retired. Harold's son and I also stay in touch. To some it seems strange to stay friendly with the competition, but like they say, "Keep your friends close and your enemy's closer." The son also wanted purchase our company, and by this time, I was interested and ready to slow it down. They had been working on almost completely changing the way they did business. It seemed to be working well for them.

Later, my son, Gary, went to work for them after the company that bought us forced him out (more on this later). I learned from him how they were approaching their sales technique, and I was intrigued.

We negotiated for months and months, and we came to the point in which we announced to all of our employees that we had sold the company to New State Industrial Products. The deal was done. They had arranged to fly all of our sales team to their company headquarters in Columbus, Ohio on the next Tuesday. We were all ready to go and meet the new company.

I felt good about the deal, and that is why I announced that we had sold the company. I had not yet signed the paperwork. I received the final copy on that Friday before our scheduled meeting, and I noticed there were some changes made to the agreement that were not there previously. In other words, they changed the deal, and I said no deal!

We went back to work Monday morning, and that was the end of that.

21

Why We Hired Some of our Salespeople

Dan Hall

I GUESS I would start with Dan Hall. Dan was the sales manager that Ron sent to train me my first days. I hired Dan because of how I felt about the sales presentation and how it had to be learned and executed by future salespeople. Dan knew the pitch better than anyone and would stick by it 100%. I was the owner, not the sales manager. I had other things to do, and I could not be with the sales team on a full-time regular basis. Dan was the choice. Over the years, many of the reps hated to work with him. If they were three minutes late picking him up in the morning, they would hear about it. As they pulled up to pick him up, he would be standing in the driveway of the hotel that he was staying at, looking down at his watch. He was a man of habit, and this is what we needed at that time. Yes, I terminated him years later, but the truth be told, he was a big part of our success and growth.

Mel S. Oklahoma City, Oklahoma.

I met Mel one morning. I only had three other interviews that day and hoped that I would meet someone that I would hire. I remember she was very professional and spoke well. She wanted to be an actress and did some local acting in town. I knew in order to be a great salesperson that you needed to be a great actor. Mel did not have a lot of sales experience, but her acting experience would make up for it. I explained that if she would follow the script (our sales presentation) she would do great. I offered her the job, and she accepted. Later we learned that she had other talents; she could write songs and sing. For several years, she would perform a new song about our company and our job at our annual year end meetings and award banquet. Everyone loved her performances, even me when she made fun of me. It was fun. Mel S. did well for herself and our company. She had nothing when I met her and when she left; she owned her own home in Oklahoma City and a second home in Denver.

Nisha S.

Nisha was a friend of one of our salespeople from that old company. She wanted to sell chemicals and was told to get a job with our company. She must have called me seven or eight times, and I said no. She didn't have any sales experience and she didn't have *IT* on the phone when we spoke. I kept saying no, but she kept calling. Finally, I agreed to meet with her in person. Virginia and I were going to San Diego to a seminar, and I made an appointment to meet with her on the way home in Orange County, California. We didn't have any salespeople in Orange County, and it would have been great to have our first. Training her would be easy as we had help that could come from LA.

Nisha interviewed in person much better than on the phone and seemed to have a hunger for money. She also had taken the time to learn quite a bit about what we did for a living and what we were going to ask her to do. This was a deciding factor. I told her that this was not a trial, or a test run that we would both be 100% committed. This is the way it had to be. I figured that anyone that would fight this hard for a job would only have to fight half as hard to ask for the order.

Nisha S. did very well. After about five years, the grass looked greener in someone else's backyard, and she decided to leave and try something different. We stayed in touch, and after a year or so she decided that the grass was not so green and came back. I guess she missed us, and the fact that she did not have to check in with someone else every day and write reports, or explain what she did and how she did it.

Being part of our company gave the sales team the opportunity to be your own boss. We did not need to know what you did every day. After all, I knew if you were working by just seeing your results. If you had them, you stayed. If you worked every day and tried your best, you stayed. If you didn't, you didn't. I was fair but consistent.

"Our success is determined by the choices we make"

Zig Ziglar & Me

22

Fundamentals of Sales

FUNDAMENTALS ARE PART OF LIFE. Whether it be on a football field or a baseball field on when they are part of your selling life, fundamentals are essential.

Coach Belichick's Patriots take the field and they are ready to play every aspect of the game; offense, defense, special teams, and kicking are all part of the plan. No matter what it took, they are prepared because they know the fundamentals of the game. Once in a while, Belichick's team would fail to play well (and that is not often). He would begin practice the following week with Lombardi-like comments: "Gentlemen, we performed below the standards we have set or ourselves as a championship team. This week we are going to return to the fundamentals."

Fundamentals remain the same, and if you analyze any leader of any organization, you will see the validity of that statement.

I have and still do believe that selling is more than a profession, it's a way of life. My concern as a leader is that all salespeople are ready for selling in these times and into the future. This means that you must be fundamentally sound and prepared to service and sell to your customers the very best, the unique, different products available to them. Always, "Sell the sizzle, not the steak."

At some point in the career of a salesperson, he or she will fall into a slump. Inevitably, when you go into a slump, you do so because you stray from the basics. With over 40 years of experience in sales from selling cars, to baby pictures, to chemicals as well as teaching people who have sold every item that you can imagine. I discovered the sure-fire way to end the slump is to return to the fundamentals with the proper attitude.

Did you know that the best paying hard work in the world is selling, also did you know that the worst paying hard work in the world is also selling?

Learn and stay with the fundamentals that you have been trained with.

———

The Move East

I think it was 1997. It was on a Saturday I called Dan Hall on the phone and said, "Dan, we are going to take a trip to Philadelphia next week."

And he said, "Ok, but why?"

I said, "Dan, we are going to start hiring salespeople there and you are going to be the vice president of sales Eastern region."

He laughed and said, "I don't think so, but I will go with you."

Dan and I were on a plane to Philadelphia the next week. I sent boxes of product samples, order pads, premiums, and everything that we would need to make sales calls to the hotels and high-rise buildings in and around the hotel that we were staying at. We were staying right in the heart of the city. This way we could walk to potential customers. Part of our task was to do the due diligence that was needed to see if starting up business in Philadelphia area was the right move at this time. We wanted to find out buying conditions in the area, who the clients bought from, what products they bought, and from who. That would tell us if gifts (premiums) were being used. We wanted to test our sales approach. Our plan was to hire salespeople and train them our way. We did notice that the maintenance people there were a little different. Philadelphians were tough and seemed rough around the edges, but if you talked to them, they were not interested in the small talk. Just get to the point. For the rest of my career when talking to the team, I would refer to the Philly customer of welcoming us with "What the F_ _ K do you want?" What an interesting way to start our pitch to him.

Another objective for the trip was to look around for a distribution warehouse that our products could be stored and shipped from. I had investigated this prior to the trip and had found a couple of public warehouses in the area. We rented a car and off we went to get the information that we needed. As it turned out, it was a very simple process. The public or commercial warehouse worked very well for all the years up until I retired. We shipped about 50 products to be stored in the Philly warehouse. We would send the orders to the warehouse via fax or e-mail. They would create the shipping documents, pull the products, and ship them with Fed X or truck. Like I said, this worked very well for many years, and to tell the truth, it was very cost affective. We could also see the inventory daily and could control it this way via their website.

We also investigated housing for Dan. He was becoming enthusiastic about this whole idea. I think it was the new title; the icing on the cake was a penthouse apartment. He loved the idea of the penthouse. It was settled. Dan was moving to Philadelphia. He was single, and he did not have many ties to San Jose. It was exciting for him to start up the company there and start up a new life. He wanted to sublet his place in San Jose and move some furniture to Philadelphia. We made a second trip to Philly soon after, and the interviewing was underway.

We interviewed Dave Dugan. Dave was looking for a sales position in outside sales. He was 6 foot 4 inches and around 300 pounds. He grew up in Vineland, New Jersey (across the river from Philadelphia). He also played football for U.C.L.A. and played for the Denver Broncos in the NFL. He was enthusiastic, upbeat, and was looking for the right company and people to work with. Remember, I was on the female kick, but I loved this guy, and so did Dan. We both thought he would get along with our kind of customer. Being so big and recognizable, he would be able to get in the door. After almost a year on the job, Dave just did not make it. He was friendly to all, but he did not have the salesperson instinct. We wished him the best and hoped he did well in the future.

Now for the redhead. She called in after seeing our ad. We decided to meet in person the following week in Philadelphia at the round Holiday Inn at city center. Let's call her Natale. She started just after Dave. I had a half dozen questions that I asked all applicants. After my first question, she answered me for ten minutes or longer. There was no stopping her. She loved to talk, but she was in charge; she had control, and taking control was the most important part of our presentation. Our salespeople had to be in control. If they lost it, they needed to get it right back pronto or they may lose the sale.

Natale loved to laugh. I told many people over the years that her laugh was contagious. Everybody loved Natale's laugh, and you could hear it all over the building. Customers used to tell me, "Oh No, there's Natale. I'm going to spend some money." They meant it affectionally. She started in July 2004. She started with nothing, no customers, no leads, just the belief that all we told her was true. I remember her first day she called me to tell me she made a sale. That's always a good sign. Natale in just a few years became the company sales leader, and for the next 12 years never gave it up. I told her many times, "You're the Best." She never complained about anything, not the products, not the office team, not even Dan Hall. She recognized that he would open her accounts and stick to the plan. She would tell that client that she would never bring him back again, that they would work with her from then on. To this day she continues to give her clients great service and respect. The east was growing in the Boston, Connecticut, and New Hampshire areas.

Dan hired in Maryland and Washington D.C. which could have gone better. We were not keeping anyone for very long, Salespeople were turning over very fast. Dan found and fell in love with the Washington D.C. area and would go there on most of his weekends, a short time later, Dan met a woman in D.C. The next thing we knew, he wanted to move there. This told me why he was having such a fast turnover rate with new salespeople. His head was up his ass and was thinking with the wrong part of his body. I agree that Dan deserved to be happy, and I was happy for him, but I also knew his track record with women. I thought this would be headed for disaster, however I agreed with the move. After a short time, his head was not 100% into his job. The lady friend did not work out, and he was distracted in his personal life and distracted on the job. We talked about it many times; I gave him several opportunities to improve his job performance. He decided to move back to California (I also did not like), and soon after I terminated him. He was not happy! He felt like I owed him more. I felt that Dan was very well paid to do the job that he did all those years. If he had been able to continue to do that job, he would have been able to keep his job; however, he did not.

Why is it that people have a tough time accepting that they are part of the problem? They always want to blame someone else. I have always said to people, "Do your job. That's all that is expected of you." This is not the end of the Dan Hall Story.

Jeanie was another of Topaz's recommendations. She came to America from Cape Town, South Africa. Another brave young woman that left her sisters, dad, and friends to have a better opportunity in America. I wanted them to succeed and was willing to do what it took to make it happen, but they had to do all the work. All I could do was give them the tools, training, product line, and support. She also started without accounts, but I remember that she had the biggest desire of all of them and the biggest chip on her shoulder. She was determined not to fail, and she was fearless. From the beginning, Jeanie called on the biggest of accounts. She sold the Los Angeles County maintenance departments, Los Angeles Unified School District maintenance departments all over the city, and there were many. She just pushed and pushed and would not take no for an answer. And soon The Yes Company was selling Los Angeles School District, the City of Los Angeles, the

County of Los Angeles, and the Los Angeles Sheriff's Department. Her sales rose from nowhere to #1 within a little more than a year. She always said, "It's about the money, just the money." No one ever wanted it more than Jeanie.

Two things happened around this time. First, the company was going to be known as The Yes Company, and second, Jeanie a few years later got married to my son, Gary.

23

The Beginning of Superco Products

ONE DAY IN 1994 JEANIE, our top salesperson in the greater Los Angeles area, came into my office and told me that she was quitting. I asked why, and she replied that she was going to go into business with her sister-in-law, Lynette, designing and selling baby clothes. I thought that was strange. She didn't even like children, and she or her sister-in-law had no experience in the baby clothing field. I told her, "I did not accept her resignation," and proceeded to tell her to go away and come back the next day and see me. I told her that I had a new idea and it included her in a big way. The next day she came in to see me, and I told her of my idea. I said that we were going to start a new company. It would be a company that would compete with this one and she was going to be both the president and an owner. She thought it over for about one second and then said yes!

We found a small warehouse and office in Culver City, California, and started the process over again. Jeanie put together the labels for Superco on her own, and she did a great job.

The company started with Jeanie, Gary, and I think one

other part-time salesperson. Gary was on his own selling full time, and Jeanie was also in the field seeing her clients. She would run the day-to-day operations, and Gary would help with training any new salespeople they hired. The storage and shipping of their orders would be done from the other company's warehouse in Burbank. Superco had a portion of the warehouse dedicated for their products. They hired a few salespeople, and we had two company's moving forward. I was still doing what I did at the old company, and Jeanie and Gary were doing their thing with Superco Products. They also hired Lynette, the sister-in-law, to sell chemicals.

In 1996, the old company had over 45 salespeople around the country. We were in about 25 of the states. Richard loved having many reps on the sales team; the problem was that some were not profitable. My argument was that I would rather have fewer sales reps that were profitable. I won. It was time to trim some fat and be more profitable.

One of my responsibilities was development of the sales team and sales management team. I also worked the product development, which meant adding new products to the line and finding other uses for products like the ceiling tile restorer.

One of the other products that I found a new use for was a vehicle undercoating spray that after spraying the undercoat of an automobile would turn into a rubberized coating to protect the underneath of the vehicle from weather. It worked well for this, but I saw it as a rubberized roof coating and patching material. As you know, this rubberized coating became very popular. We were the first with it. I sure missed the boat with this product as far as the big picture was concerned. I am sure that all of you have seen the advertisement with the guy cutting in half the rowboat then patching it with the rubberized coating. Guess where he got that idea? Our next great new and different product was the cleaning sponge. I found it online and found a distributor to buy it from China and sell it to us for the first year. It also became a product on our top ten list. Our sales team could sell products that other companies did not have or offer. This gave us a huge advantage over the competition.

Another part of my job was developing the sales team and overseeing that all were profitable. The number of salespeople that you have is great, but they need to make money for themselves and for the company. For over 20 years, I was on an airplane somewhere in America doing just that. I worked long hours, and I spent many weekends away from home, interviewing new salespeople. We had gone from 1.6 million dollars in sales to 8 million in sales. Richard's job was to oversee the office team this included shipping, purchasing, collections, etc. He handled the inside, and I worked the outside. After 18 years, I was not happy with how he handled his part. He was late paying bills, and we were out of stock too often, which made shipments to clients late. It was now time for me and Richard to get a divorce. In December 1999, we split up.

The deal was he kept AIS, and I took over Superco. I also kept 10 salespeople that were with the old company. I also received a buyout for my interest in the old company. He had to make payments as he claimed he had no money. I picked the 10 salespeople that I wanted and off we went. Not really. I picked the 10 that I wanted to take with me, and he talked some of them out of leaving, telling them that I had no chance of making it alone. We had to change the deal and tell anyone I wanted that they had no choice. Not to my surprise, when I left in 2017 to retire, eight of the 10 remained with me. The ex-partner lost most of his people; some left him to join us. Others got out of the business. Not to mention he went bankrupt two times and is now long gone. I guess I did make it on my own after all!

It was important to continue to treat the sales team as if they were the greatest in the world, and they were. We always would reach out to them when they did something good. If a salesperson had a great day or opened a big new account that they had been working on, we would call them and congratulate them, and then send them a gift certificate or some free premiums. It was very important that they knew we appreciated them. If a new salesperson had a sale on their first day in the field alone, their sales manager or I would call them up and congratulate them and tell them to take their spouse or significant other out to dinner to their favorite restaurant and send the bill into the office. It was important to make sure that they felt special whenever possible. Perhaps this was another reason that they stayed with us for so long.

After we split, we needed a new home office and a warehouse for Superco. I leased a small unit in Valencia, California, my hometown. This meant no freeways for me anymore.

24

I Had No Idea What I Had Gotten Myself Into!

ONCE AGAIN, I was starting over. First, we had to set up the company for the 10 veteran salespeople. Both the customers and the salespeople expected to order and receive their products in a few days, as always. They all left the old company on a Friday and started with us the following Monday morning. They were told that everything would run smoothly and that their customers would not notice anything different. They were telling their customers that they now worked with Superco Products, and Superco was a sister company to AIS all these years. All the products were to be the same; even the product code numbers are the same, which they were. Only the name of the product was different; all of this was 100% true. With some help from Jeanie and Tom (computer person), we had to hire someone to help us run the office and hire an office team. It seemed that there were like a million things that had to get done, and all of them had to get done now, including finding a new warehouse. The warehouse needed equipment, including a forklift, and racks stocked full of product to ship. We also had to hire an experienced warehouse person.

We purchased a new computer system and all the data had to be input, including customer information, product codes etc. Whoa, what a job!

All the salespeople that came to Superco from the old company kept their original agreements; they were grandfathered in. They were paid without interruption. For the first six months, Virginia and I received zero pay. In fact, we used the payments coming in from the old company to keep us paying our personal expenses.

About this time, I began to have neck pain, migraines, and other issues. There is something to be said for stress. But all was great; I loved what I was doing.

The second six months of the first year were better. Sales were going upward, and customers were paying their invoices. We had a great office and warehouse team (so I thought), until we discovered the warehouse people were stealing inventory. They got fired and prosecuted. We had to hire and train new warehouse staff and put in security cameras. I trusted everyone, and once again rule #2 came into play.

Rule #2: "Once you think you have met the biggest thief, liar, or cheat there will be a bigger one coming down the road in the future." You can bet on it.

Sometime around 2005, three Midwest salespeople that were still working for Richard at the old company contacted me. They wanted to leave him and return to work for me. All were from Saint Louis, Missouri, and all were experienced salespeople. The leader was a very talented sales manager who had been with the old company for quite a while. The second was a very average salesperson and did not stay long with us. The third was Marissa Lang. I did not know her very well; she was hired just around the time that I left the old company.

I got a chance to know Marissa. She became very loyal, and I love loyalty almost as much as President Trump does. Her sales were average, but her work habits were fantastic. She had a way with working with other salespeople and the office team. Her clients loved her, and they were loyal. She also understood the products and how they worked to help the customers. She had a knack to get people to do things for her because they wanted to, and not because they had to. People like to work with her.

After a year or so, I asked her to join a management team and to develop the Midwest Region. Her motivation to succeed was that she wanted to do it for others, not solely for herself. I have seen this before. When Marissa worked with her reps in the field, their sales were far better that her own. Her personal sales over the years got much better.

Marissa asked if she could hire a rep in Kansas City (about 50 minutes by air from STL) as her first city. I did the interviewing with her. Together we decided which two would we fly to Saint Louis where she would do the observation day. She then would pick the candidate that she felt would have the best chance of making it. I found that the Midwest had a very different customer personality than anywhere that I have ever worked. They were nicer, easier to get along with, and would often invite you in to see them without a battle. When I went to work in the field with her, I noticed the customers did not warm up to my personality or way of selling. We decided that it may be best for her to do as much as possible and for me to stand off.

We used to say you don't know what's behind any door. That's why you should go through the door to find out. Marissa went through a door one day in a very little town in southern Illinois that led her to a huge account that to this day orders 50,000 dollars in product every year.

Marissa took the concept of our sales presentation and used it in a way that it worked for both her and the customers. She used our sales presentation, but presented them in her way. We added two new points to the presentation. Seeing how this worked was one of the best things that happened to our company. Marissa went on to build a 100 thousand-dollar territory into a 1.5 million-dollar region in just a few years. In the next three years, she had salespeople in Chicago, Oklahoma City, Dallas, Houston, Nashville, Kansas City, Fort Lauderdale, and a couple more in Saint Louis. She was doing a great job, but this did not define her to me as a person. Her next greatest challenge was about to begin.

By this time, she got married and had two children, a boy and a baby girl. When Emmie was maybe one-year-old or so, doctors found tumors in her head. Wow! Marissa and Justin spent most of their time at the hospital. Emme had to go through operations, chemo, and god knows what else. It was hell for her family. We did the best we could; we supported them as much as we could. We had "Emme Friday" once a month. Whatever was sold by the entire company that Friday, we donated a percentage to the Emmie Fund. That money went to Marissa, and she donated it to the Saint Louis Children's Hospital. The last time I spoke to her, all is well in their home, and Emme was five years old and doing great. What a miracle. It pays to be a nice person.

To go through something like this, I cannot imagine. She was so strong. She did very little travel for work, if any, but she still had to see her customers and talk on the phone to all her sales-reps for hours every week. I told her that she is one of the strongest women I have ever known.

One of her sales gals came to her from Houston, Texas,

Barbara Levy. I met and interviewed her and Angie in Texas while recruiting new salespeople. I hired both. Angie was a great hire. She had it all, but she had one problem. She was going to sell our products her way and was not going to listen to anyone. She reminded me of me, stubborn and talented. She was going to succeed her way. She did, and when I retired, she was still there and having her best year ever.

On the other hand, Barbara followed the sales presentation and believed in it. They both started with nothing, no customers, no leads, no nothing. I have respect for anyone that can do this. And they both stayed and succeeded. The difference is that Barbara's husband, Johnathan, decided he wanted to leave Houston and move back to south Florida where they lived before and were close to Johnathan's mother. We hired a new person to take over her accounts in Houston, and she had to start over again, developing a new account base and territory in the greater Fort Lauderdale area. This time she got very little help in the field. She did it by herself. I could not imagine anyone succeeding in two territories from the ground up, and yet we had two salespeople able to achieve this remarkable challenge. She too was still working in Florida when I retired. We stay in touch and she still calls me the "Big Kahuna." It's been a lot of fun and a pleasure to know and work with her.

One of the things that always bothered me when I was at the old company and had a partner, is that we never seem to get ahead with money or the account payables. Often one of the suppliers would call me and ask for a payment. This was not my responsibility, it was Richard's. I hated these calls, and like I said, we were selling millions of dollars of product, and we seemed to be broke.

It did not take long after our divorce and I took over

Superco that The Yes Company had a very nice balance in its checkbook.

I don't think we ever paid a bill late unless somehow it may have gotten lost. Our credit rating was as high as it could be, along with a large-dollar line of credit with our bank. What can I say, splitting up with my partner was the best thing that I ever did for all of us? Things were going very well.

Once again, we moved a couple of blocks to a much larger home office and warehouse. Superco stayed there until I left.

I had an office manager that was with us for over nine years. She had a great relationship with both the sales team and her office team. Late into her eighth year, things took a turn, and I began to get calls from people and things did not add up. Here we go again; rule # 2.

I started to investigate what was going on. Bills were not being paid, and multiple state sales tax collections were not up to date. She would tell a salesperson that she would do something and not get it done. She stole from us to the tune of about 150,000 to 200,000 dollars. This was all my fault. This is what happens when you let people do their job, believe in them, and do not check up on them. Once again you think you have seen it all, and they bite you in the ass. Always another one coming around the corner, Watch your back!

I talked to the Santa Clarita sheriff's department. They did an investigation and turned it over to the prosecutor's office, who told me it was not worth them prosecuting. It was too small. As far as I was concerned, they were very proud of the fact that they had a reputation that Santa Clarita had a very low crime rate. Maybe this is the way they kept it that way. I never did understand.

About a year and a half later, I received a call for another business owner in the area who had hired the same woman that stole from us and in a short time. She embezzled much more from them than from us. He did have a case; she committed identity fraud. She had the employees' credit and bank information and used it to acquire money and make credit card purchases. Thank goodness she did not do this to us. She was prosecuted, found guilty, and received three years in California state prison. I guess the city was more excited to prosecute for the identity fraud. She got what she had coming.

In my career, I always talked about attitude and keeping it positive. Through the years, we went through the "R" word (recession) twice, in 1982 and 2008. In fact, we started the old company during a recession. All you read or heard from the news was, "Oh my God, everything is bad." The stock market was down, and unemployment was high. No cars were being purchased. No industrial equipment was being purchased. Everything was looking bad. At least that is what the newspapers and television news reported. Well, guess what? This couldn't be better for us. It was not that I wanted to see the country in a recession. Throughout the recessions, I preached that recession is good for the specialty chemical industry. It was good for our company and for us. We are in the business of selling maintenance and chemical products to all the businesses that are being told the country is slowing down. I guess they had "Fake News" then as well.

All our customers were being told by the higher ups not to spend money on capital purchases. They were being told to make good with what they had. They had to repair, clean, lubricate, and maintain all their equipment, property, vehicles, etc. They were not going to put on a new roof; they would now order our roofing materials to maintain the existing roof. This is what we do; we sell products to maintain their existing equipment. They could not buy new air conditioners. They were maintaining the old ones. Plumbing, painting, and cleaning everything. This was a really good time for The Yes Company. Not to mention the unemployment rate was very high at somewhere around 9%. This meant there was a large pool of potential great salespeople out there. We just had to find the ones that wanted to work and didn't feel entitled. In 2009, it was time to grow again.

We were and still are doing different things and offering benefits to potential salespeople that most other companies were not.

- Higher commissions 32 to 37%
- All expensive paid trips to places such as Caribbean and Mexican Cruises, New Orleans, Florida, Las Vegas and many others. These trips were for sales contest winners and a guest.
- Auto Allowance
- Premium Allowance
- Medical, dental and Vision benefits (We paid a percentage based on the salespersons sales per year.)

We were looking for salespeople in the west and the east. The east was now being managed from Connecticut by my son, Scott. Remember Ann and Don from Connecticut that came with Howard from Atlanta? Ann married Scott. Ann is great, always does a good job, and never complains about anything. It seems that she is just happy to have her job. We had a couple of people in the east, but we wanted to add more.

In 2006, I got a phone call from a veteran salesperson

that lived in the western part of Massachusetts about 50 miles from Boston. She was selling for a company that was making promises and not keeping them. The company had a reputation of being very aggressive, similar to us. Their salespeople were well trained and disciplined. She was not happy with several things, including the structure and management's style. She worked directly with the owner. We shared some same customers, and apparently those customers told her about us. That's how she came to call me. We spoke on the phone, and I felt like it was worth a trip to Boston to meet with her. It also gave me a chance to visit with some of my relative's that lived in Boston.

I grew up in Boston. On my father's side, I had many aunts, uncles, and cousins. This was a great opportunity to visit.

Sharon G. and I decided to meet at a hotel in the Boston area in a week. From our phone conversations, I could tell that Sharon G. was very focused on making money and being #1 with us or anyone that she was employed with. She asked me who was our #1 salesperson. I told her the redhead in Philadelphia and that being 2nd to her was ok. She planned on being number one in the future. Sharon G. is the mother of two daughters. She is one of the most money motivated people I have ever met. This became one of my most intense negotiations ever, and to be fair, Sharon G. won.

First understand that The Yes Company paid more commission than anyone in the industry. We paid 32% compared to other companies that paid from 25% to 30%. We also gave the opportunity to earn 35% or 37% depending on how high your sales volume was. Sharon's commission stayed the same, she always was in the 35% or more tier. She also wanted more auto allowance, premium allowance, and insurance allowance. I agreed to give it to her if she achieved certain goals that I set for her. I remember that one July she sold over 65,000 dollars in a single month. It was a sales record for our company. As I suspected, Sharon G. sold as much as 475,000 dollars a year for twelve years with us. Most reps sold around 175,000 dollars to 225,000 dollars. It was great having her come to our company; it was a great deal for both of us. Sharon G. always worked very hard; no one gave her anything. She earned everything that she had, and I could not feel prouder. There was an award given out each year for the salesperson that opened the most new accounts in the year. I am sure that Sharon won this most years. I remember many phone calls to me from Sharon about products and product recommendations. These calls would come from her at six in the morning while she was on her way to the first sales call of the day. Some calls came at 6 p.m. while she was on her way home from work. After all, sales are not going to come to you, you need to go out and see the customers in person. Most reps that failed didn't seem to get this concept. They thought that the customer would call them and give them an order over the phone. They also would go home early and start late. These types of salespeople did not stay with us very long.

25

Company Perks

Year End Meetings

WHILE WRITING THIS, I decided to contact some of my past associates and ask if there were any personal things that they wanted to share with me. Many responded with the same thoughts. It seemed that they all enjoyed the company year-end meetings and the company trips.

The first year-end meeting was at the Westin Hotel, Los Angeles Airport Hotel in 1984. I remember it like it was yesterday. I wanted it to go perfectly. I wanted all that attended to have a great time. Each salesperson had their own room; all expenses were paid, including cocktails at the banquet. We changed this later due to a little too many cocktails. The men wore tuxedos and the women gowns. You would think we were going to the Oscars. I had made all the arrangements, from hotel reservations, to the rooms that we were going to have our meetings in. I oversaw everything. I even made sure that Dan and Richard knew what they were expected to do and how to do it. Guess I over managed. Later, I backed off a lot. Our office manager and our sales managers pretty much did it all. The office manager made all the air and hotel reservations including meeting rooms, food and beverage; the sales managers did everything that was needed for the sales meetings, including seminars. I reviewed new products with them, and they both did a fantastic job.

The year-end meetings were important to the management team, and I know the sales team enjoyed them. This is where they got the recognition that they deserved for the prior year's work and sales achievements. They received awards from "Rookie of the Year" to "Sale's Volume Leader" to "Salesperson of the Year." There were sales plateaus set up; we called them the *Plateaus to Success*. Most salespeople enjoy the opportunity to reach a challenge and then be rewarded in front of their peers. Each plateau that they reached, they were rewarded with a bonus check. This bonus ranged from 750 dollars to 5000 dollars.

The sales people that reached the highest plateau along with the cash award received a gold and diamond ring in the shape of our logo. You can imagine how motivating this was to be one of the very few with the company diamond ring.

Company Trips

Our goal was for the trips to go even better than the meetings. The sales contest winners who were attending were the leaders of the company. Virginia and I wanted them to feel very special. The trip destination was carefully chosen, and we would make the announcement of the trip at the year-end banquet. We held a six-month contest. Each sales-rep was given a quota, and our goal was that everyone would win. Approximately 60% of the sales team earned the trip each year. I do remember we broke the rules and invited a few to join, even without qualifying that year.

Speaking of rules, we had very few. I remember telling people during interviews, "If you're looking for corporate America, we are not it." This seemed to interest many of our applicants. However, we did have a few rules that needed enforcing. One of them regarding the protection of accounts. Some say we didn't do a good job at this one once in a while. They were the one on the losing end. Sorry. But when it came to rules about the trips, we broke them on occasion.

One of our past associates wrote that one of the most memorable trips was to Mexico at an all-inclusive resort in Cancun. Virginia thought that we should do a special dinner on the beach the last night of our stay. So, we contacted catering, and they put on quite a wonderful dinner for all of us under the moonlight on the beach. The fact that it was remembered as a special night makes it all worth it for us. We loved to please our employees, and we tried very hard.

Most of our friends from the past said that what they liked about working with us was the fact that they were not over managed and could go at their pace. No reports, no checkups, just pretty much left alone. However, some did say that they knew that if they ever needed anything, they felt very comfortable coming to us and asking for help or support. I hope that's why so many stayed with us for as long as they did.

Part of the Family

I sent out an e-mail to some salespersons, asking them for their memories of their time spent with us. Many answered that they enjoyed my humor at sales meetings and in the field when I had the pleasure to ride with them visiting customers. I did say visiting, but I really meant making sales calls. I always reminded everyone that the only reason to see a client was for customer service, but always make a sale call out of it. You were not there to visit.

Some past associates remarked that they enjoyed that my mother, stepfather, and Virginia's mother and father came to year end meetings. They even came on some sales contest trips. We enjoyed having them be part of the company, and they loved being able to attend and meet and visit with all the sales and office teams. It was great fun, and everybody felt much more a part of the family.

26

Interesting and Different Sales Calls in the Field

United States Navy Base, San Diego, California

I WAS WORKING with an Alco Products salesperson, Mel Garber. I was a sales manager for them at the time. We were going to see his best account, the navy base in San Diego. Our first sales call was to a couple of tenders (repair ships). Tenders would go out to sea to do maintenance work on ships that were out to sea. Sometimes they would work on an aircraft carrier or a battleship. Carriers and battleships had their own maintenance crews on board. The tenders were like specialty personnel. The highlight was that we got to go on the Coral Sea aircraft carrier. For me, this was an unbelievable experience. We not only got to make sales, we got a tour of the carrier. It saw thousands of seamen and pilots who worked on it and fought on it. It had jet planes. It was something. We made money and had a great time.

Slippery Rock University, Slippery Rock, Pennsylvania

Slippery Rock got on the map in the 1990s by having a sensational track and field athlete that was featured on ESPN Sports shows and the newspapers. It seemed that they had a story about this athlete every week, and I think he came from Slippery Rock University.

I was working with Kathleen M., a salesperson that lived and worked in Pittsburg, Pennsylvania. She graduated from the University of West Virginia. She wanted to call on her old school's maintenance department. She remembered a few of the maintenance workers, and she thought she could sell them some of our products. I said, "Ok, let's go." On the way, there was a sign on the highway that said, "Slippery Rock University 16 miles." I told her I wanted to go there first. I just wanted to see the school after hearing about it all this time. I was excited to see it and buy a tee shirt or a hat. When we arrived, we went straight to the physical plant where we found *Archie Bunker*. As I remember, he was very happy to see us. I guess he didn't get many visitors out there in the middle of nowhere. We demonstrated a few products to him, and I then asked him for the order and he said yes. We then headed to the student store to shop. I bought a Slippery Rock hat. It was fun, and we made the sale. I don't think she ever sold the client again (she never went back). We did go to West Virginia University and make several sales. Kathleen made them herself with very little help from me.

Washington National Cathedral, Washington D.C.

Maybe the most beautiful building I have ever seen is the Washington National Cathedral. I was working with Julie, a sales-rep we had with the old company in Washington DC. I said, "Let's go to the Washington National Cathedral."

She said, "No way. We will never get in to see anyone, we are just wasting our time."

Now I wanted to go even more. When we arrived, we decided to look around and see the building. While doing so, we spotted a worker making a repair. We asked him who was in charge of the maintenance department, and where was he located? He said that his name was Bob Jamison. He was about to get on the radio, but I stopped him and said just tell us where he hangs out. "Where is his office located?" He decided he would take us there. Once we got there, I told him thank you and said that we would handle it from there.

"Why did you stop him from using the radio and excuse the man that brought us here?" Julie asked me when we got back to the car.

I responded, "If he gets the boss on the radio he will ask, 'who is it and what do they want?' Then he will say he's busy and get rid of us." I continued to explain that I was sure this happened to many sales reps thousands of times. As for asking him to go away in the sales presentation, *getting them alone is crucial.* Remember? It's best to pitch alone. Bob was a very friendly person, and after we showed him rust stain remover that worked on concrete, he ordered it and some carpet stain remover for around 800 dollars. It was a very nice first-time sale. Julie went on and sold him for years to come.

I asked her, "Where else do you not want to go to?"

Richard H Donavan Federal Prison, San Diego, California

This account was opened by a salesperson named Rita. She met the director of maintenance, Dave S. who worked at the prison, at one of the many trade shows that we exhibited our products at over the years. I called Rita and asked if she minded that I spend a day in the field with her. I wanted to go with her to the prison as an observer. She set an appointment with her client for the next week. Before I could go with her, I had to go through a very extensive background check in order to get a pass. I filled out all the paperwork and sent it in to the prison. It all got approved.

The next week, Rita and I were at the prison to see her customer. We arrived and waited in the waiting room for Dave S. to see us, but he sent an escort to bring us to him. There were two of them. One worked for the prison and the other was an inmate. As we were walked through the halls and through a large courtyard, there was a lot of whistling and cat calls coming our way, and I am pretty sure they were not for me. Rita was a very attractive young woman. She had been talking to Dave S. about our drain maintenance products. They were very interested in the kitchen areas of the buildings. The kitchen drains often had grease build up that would cause the drains to drain slowly or to back up. We had a solution. They needed Gobble, a de-Limonin based product that safely dissolved the hydrocarbons (grease) and the foodstuff in the drain lines, allowing them to flow clearly and freely.

By using Gobble through automated chemical dispensers (Superco Drain Maintainer) we knew that their problems would be gone. After a visual demonstration of Gobble, Dave S. placed an order for two 55-gallon containers, and we gave him the automatic drain dispenser at no charge. The initial order came to about 5,600 dollars. This business and much more stayed with us for several years until Rita mysteriously left.

This was just a few of the interesting places that I visited over the years, and there were many more. What a great job sales is!

27

Making Proper Choices

UNDERSTANDING THE DIFFERENCE BETWEEN
REACTING AND RESPONDING TO SITUATIONS

Zig's Story

IN JANUARY 1992, Zig was in Kansas City. He was doing a recording session for one of his tapes. Yes, in those days they did tapes. They had a 3 p.m. flight back to Dallas where he lived. He had to hurry because the airline said to be there one hour early. He got to the airport at 2 PM and went to the counter. There were long lines waiting to check in. He noticed one ticket agent walked behind the counter that had a sign that said, "position closed." However, he knew that would open soon, so he waited there. Sure enough, she took down the sign and announced, "Anyone here on the 3 p.m. flight to Dallas?" Well Zig was first in line, and the ticket agent looked at him, smiled, and said, "The 3 O'clock flight to Dallas has been cancelled."

Zig enthusiastically responded, **"FANTASTIC!"**

With a puzzled look on her face, the agent asked, "Now why in the world would you say 'fantastic' when I just told you that your flight was canceled?"

Zig responded with, "Ma'am there are only three

reasons that flight would cancel. Number one, something must be wrong with the airplane. Number two, something must be wrong with the person who's going to fly it. Or number three. Something must be wrong with the weather that they are going to fly that airplane in. Now Ma'am, if anyone of those situations exist, I don't want to be up there! I want to be right down here. So **FANTASTIC.**"

The lady looked at him and said, "I am really puzzled. Why in the world would you say 'fantastic' when I just told you that you have a four hour wait in the Kansas City airport?"

He smiled back at her and said, "It's really very simple. I'm 54 years old and never before in my entire life have I had the opportunity to spend four hours in the Kansas City airport." He continued, "Don't you realize at this moment, there are tens of millions of people on this earth, who are not only cold, but hungry? Here I am in a beautiful build- ing, and even though it's cold outside, it's very comfortable inside. Down the hallway is a nice little coffee shop. I'm going to go down there, have a nice cup of coffee, relax a few minutes, and then I have some very important work which I need to do. I am in one of the nicest buildings in the area: It's comfortable, rent-free offices, and at my disposal. **FANTASTIC!**"

That's strong, even for a positive speaker. Moral to the story. You have an opportunity to **REACT** which is negative or to **RESPOND** which is positive. The choice is yours. It's a fact that you can't **tailor make** the situations in life, but you can tailor make your attitude to fit the situation. All of life is a series of choices, and it's what you choose to give life today that will determine what life will give you tomorrow. You can choose to get drunk tonight, but when you do, you have chosen to feel miserable tomorrow. This is the message

I'm giving you. You are free to choose, but the choices you make today will determine what you will have, be, and do in the tomorrows of your life. You can choose to take the necessary steps to help you succeeded as a salesperson, or you can choose to ignore the experience of successful leaders and managers and take the consequences for yourself. You must learn that you are responsible for your attitude. Every choice that we make, whether it is good or bad, has consequences.

Back to the airport. He had another choice he could have ranted and raved, screamed and made a scene. He could have made a fool of himself and embarrassed everybody around him by screaming, "That's Crazy. That's Nuts. I'm Tired. It's Friday, I want to get home! I've been gone all week! Who made this decision anyway? Who runs this airline?" Yes, he could have chosen that as a second reaction. Guess what. The next flight still doesn't leave for four hours.

When you go out into the field and meet a client who is abusive to you and treats you like dirt, you have the choice how to respond to him. Take my advice. Smile, leave, and go on to the next lucky person who is going to have the opportunity to buy from you and use our wonderful products.

The choice is yours.

28

Final Words of Wisdom

Your company will sell itself on its name and reputation.

CUSTOMERS WANT to deal with a reputable company with name recognizable products, but most of all you need to be in a position where he wants to buy from you. A great salesperson must believe in their products. Use the products you sell at home. This will help you get sold on the products, and you can tell your customers that you use them at home and often recommend them to friends and relatives. This will help you in being more convincing and easily persuaded.

Positive Attitude must always be used

I don't ever recall meeting a successful anybody that did not have a positive mental attitude. Attitude is Contagious. In order to be a success, you must believe that you will sell to every person you ever talk to. When you believe that you will close every sale, you will discover that your percentage rate will increase. When you walk into a customer's office with a spring in your step or the dragging of your feet. Your smile, the inflection of your voice, the way you stand, and your body language will communicate how you feel about yourself. If you are down, take a break, call someone that can help, call a friend, or worst case, take the rest of the day off.

You're no good to anyone feeling down and out. If you're down three days in a row and it's about your sales job, get a new job!

Always be Prepared

Never enter a sales presentation unprepared. Know everything about your products, your customers, his business, your competition. Attend seminars, read sales magazines. Go to Barnes and Noble bookstore; they have hundreds of books on sales, motivation, self-help, negotiating the sale, and having a positive mental attitude.

I recommend that you read both *The Secrets Power Negotiating* by Rodger Dawson and *IACOCCA: An Autobiography* by Lee Iacocca.

Have constructive conversations with other salespeople, not bull sessions. Exchange idea's with top salespeople in your field. Exchange leads with other salespeople within your account base. They may be selling something other than what you sell. Have a cup of coffee or go to lunch with them, exchange customers with them. Be an expert. There is no excuse for you to be anything less.

Never discuss politics or religion! Have your business card state your accomplishments at your company i.e. Rookie of the Year, Top Salesperson, Salesperson of the year, etc.

Always be sincere and Don't make promises you can't keep.

#1 Rule: don't make any promises you can't keep. If you do, and then don't do what you say you were going to do, **you lose!**

Be sincere and honest, never lie to a customer.

If a customer asked you a question and you're unable to answer it, tell him you'll get back to him right away. Call your manager or the office and get the answer to his question and get right back to him.

Always Assume the Sale.

Use those subtle statements for assuming the sale while going through the presentation.

"Do you prefer UPS or Fed X? I'll send the invoice to your attention."

"It's a great idea to order today before the price increase."

"I will be sure that the products are delivered by next week."

Remember to know the answer to any question that you may ask him/her. You can get yourself into a lot of trouble without knowing the answer before you ask. Never ask a question during the close that requires a "yes" or "no" answer unless you are positive that it is a "yes." Don't ask, do you want me to ship the products today? Instead, you should ask, "Do you want all of it shipped this month, or would rather I ship part now and part later to better fit your budget?"

Get in the habit of using the words "Don't you agree"? For Instance, "Don't you agree that this works great? Don't you agree Mr. Customer that this is something that you can really use?" This way you're asking the customer to agree with you on questions that will get you a YES response. This is a kind of reverse Agree, Agree, Agree.

Get your customers to take part in the demonstration of the products. They love it. You will want them to get used to owning the product by making them a part of the demo; they feel ownership. Once a customer feels ownership, closing the sale becomes a formality. A great salesperson gets the customer involved and then watches for the moment when he shows satisfaction by his body language or the sparkle in his eye. Now is your chance to say, "Your boss is going to be very happy with you when he sees the result of how these products perform." He will visualize all this happening because you painted the right mental picture.

Remember, never take your customers for granted.

Conclusion

After 36 years, I began to lose a little interest in the company and came up with a 5-year exit plan. In 2012, Gine and I moved to Las Vegas and started a new chapter. I began to explore selling the company. Over the next four years, I went through the process of selling Superco two times. I got far into the process. In fact, I mentioned earlier that we had a done deal until the very last day, and I pulled out.

In January 2017, I received a call from someone who identified himself as a principle of a company from Georgia. After a few conversations with him, the president of the company called me. He gave me their history. They are an old company and are direct competitors to us. I had not heard of them. I talked to friends in the industry and asked about this company. Everyone that I talked to said that they had a good reputation. After talking to them for several weeks, they invited me to visit them. I agreed.

When I got to their office, they were very inviting, and I got the grand tour. I saw the warehouse and the manufacturing plant. I met the large office team with the many vice presidents. I even noticed the walls in the main hallway had pictures of their sales team. We also had our walls covered with our sales team and the sales trip vacations. They were very much like us and seemed to have the same philosophies. The sales team came first. They had over 100 salespeople and many for a very long time, just like us. Their president was an old gentleman whose father started the company almost 50 years ago. The CEO was his son, who mostly listened, and the president did most of the talking and promising. They gave me a letter of intent and after a short time, Gine and I accepted the offer.

In August 2017, they brought all our salespeople to Atlanta. The agreements (contracts) that each salesperson had with Superco were promised to stay the same, the customers would stay the same, the perks would all stay the same. On September 1, 2017, I was out of a job for the first time since I was 16 years old. I had sold the company. I have no airplanes to catch and no meetings to go to. I made mistakes, and I learned a lot. While all didn't go as planned, all is good, and life is good.

I wish you all the best! Good luck and good selling,
Steve

Acknowledgments

I want to thank the people that helped me with my life and my journey. First my wife Virginia, who was there when we first started and would do anything without being asked. Virginia is the rock of our family. Next, my three sons, Gary, Scott, and Randy, who worked hard every day to please me and the company for well over 20 years each. I am very proud of all that they have accomplished. I would also like to thank the sales management teams and all the salespeople and office staff, some of which were with us for 10, 20, even 30 years. Without them there would never have been any of this.

Good Luck and Good Selling,

Steve Cina

About the Author

Steve Cina resides in Las Vegas, Nevada with his wonderful wife Virginia. He keeps busy during retirement by traveling, golfing, and watching his grandson, Brady, play baseball.

CPSIA information can be obtained
at www.ICGtesting.com
Printed in the USA
FSHW010127180420
69274FS